MIX
Papier aus verantwortungsvollen Quellen
Paper from responsible sources
FSC® C105338

Manuel Müller

Crossing Borders

European Cooperation for success

Anchor Compact

Müller, Manuel: Crossing Borders: European Cooperation for success. Hamburg, Diplomica Verlag GmbH 2012
Original title of the thesis: Crossing boarders Cooperation for a strong united Europe

ISBN: 978-3-95489-014-9
Print: Anchor Academic Publishing, an Imprint of Diplomica® Verlag GmbH, Hamburg, 2012
Additionally: Diplomica Verlag GmbH, Hamburg, Deutschland, Bachelor Thesis, 2011

Bibliographical Information of the German National Library:
The German National Library lists this publication in the German National Bibliography. Detailed bibliographic data can be found at: http://dnb.d-nb.de

The digital publication (eBook) of this work with the ISBN 978-3-95489-514-4 can be purchased on the general market or directly from the publisher.

Table of Content

LIST OF FIGURES VII

LIST OF TABLES VIII

ABBREVIATION INDEX IX

1 INTRODUCTION 11

2 EDUCATION & TRAINING 13

2.1 Introduction and General Information 13

The Lisbon Strategy 15

The Bologna Process 16

2.2 Life-long learning Program 2007-2013 24

3 CENTRAL EUROPE – COOPERATION FOR SUCCESS 34

3.1 Introduction 34

3.2 Goals and Direction 45

3.3 SoNorA – South North Axis 57

4 CONCLUSION AND OUTLOOK 61

LIST OF REFERENCES AND SOURCES 65

APPENDIX 73

List of Figures

Figure 1: Knowledge Triangle 18
Figure 2: Pisa reading literacy scale 20
Figure 3: Budget Evolution per Sub-program 32
Figure 4: CENTRAL EUROPE Program Area 35
Figure 5: Landscape and settlement structures, 2007 37
Figure 6: GDP per Capita 2007 (NUTS3) 41
Figure 7: 5 major trans-European transport axes 44
Figure 8: SOuth-NORth-Axis Project partner map 57

List of Tables

Table 1: Pisa survey, low reading skills................................22

Table 2: Outgoing Erasmus Students Under the Life-long Learning Program 2007/08 2009/10..28

Table 3: Year by source for the program (in EUR)...............55

Table 4: Priority axes by source of funding. 56

Abbreviation Index

CEI	- Central European Initiative
CEP	- Central Europ Programme
CO2	- Carbon Dioxide
ECTS	- European Credit Transfer System
ERDF	- European Research & Development Fund
ET	- Education and Training
EU	- European Union
EUR	- Euro (Currency)
FDI	- Foreign Direct Investment
GDP	- Gross Domestic Product
HEIs	- Higher Education Institutes
ICT	- Information and Communication Technology
ISO	- International Organisation for Standardisation
LLP	- Life-long Learning Programme
NUTS	- Nomenclature des Unités Territoriales Statistiques
R&TD	- Research & Technology Development
SDS	- Sustainable Development Strategy
SONORA	- South-North-Axis
TEN-T	- Trans-European Transport Network
UNESCO	- United Nations Educational, Scientific & Cultural Organisation
VET	- Vocational Education & Training

1 Introduction

The European Union has until now delivered peace, prosperity and stability for half a century. Economic cooperation has been on the first steps being fostered. As a result the conflicts among economically independent countries had been able to reduce. Nowadays the European Union is not anymore only a partnership of countries, but also a single market. Another result of the globalization relating to free movement of goods, services, people and capital is the risen standard of living.

With the aim of achieving one strong and competitive economic area the first aim has to be reaching one equal standard among all countries. This means to support and help disadvantaged countries to develop and reduce their deficits but also ensure sustainable growth without limiting the opportunities for future plans. One of the keys for successful and sound growth without restricting future possibilities is trans-national cooperation. In terms of competition the only aim is to be more productive and generate more added values. Within international cooperation every participant can benefit from knowledge or expertise exchange and learn more about cultural diversity.

Deficits can be seen in various areas from highly developed Information and Communication Technologies to basic supply as sufficient Infrastructure networks e.g. roads or railroads. In order to reduce those deficits the European Union is supporting numerous programmes and projects in every possible field.

As one part of this thesis I will introduce the 'Education and Training' sector of the EU and give a general overview of the Lisbon Strategy and Bologna Process. The main part of the Education and Training programmed is the Life-long

Learning Programme. Implemented in 2007 the structures, action plans and aims are responsible to lead Europe to a more connected future and an improved education and training system. Further the different areas of the LLP (Life-long Learning Programme) are explained which are ensuring that not only single parts of the system are promoted but every sector of the education and training system is facilitated.

As one part of this thesis I will introduce the 'Education and Training' sector of the EU and give a general overview of the Lisbon Strategy and Bologna Process. The main part of the Education and Training programme is the Life-long Learning Programme. Implemented in 2007 the structures, action plans and aims are responsible to lead Europe to a more connected future and an improved education and training system. Further the different areas of the LLP (Life-long Learning Programme) are explained which are ensuring that not only single parts of the system are promoted but every sector of the education and training system is facilitated.
In the end of the paper there is a conclusion about status and development of the highlighted areas and projects in the chapters before. Purpose of the thesis in general is to figure out if new member states, Central Europe countries supported by established program can catch up to the western countries of the European Union. In possible terms of an open answer to this question and still targeting a competitive economy, considerations may be necessary about alternative investments with higher benefits. As part of the elaboration a survey has been created, relating on the partially underdeveloped infrastructure and the decreasing population numbers in new member states. Results of this survey are included to allocate reasons for the negative development and are featured within the conclusion.

2 Education & Training

2.1 Introduction and General Information

"Education, training and youth play an essential role in a knowledge-based economy as they support growth and employment by encouraging the emergence of a highly qualified and adaptable population. They also strengthen social cohesion and active citizenship within the European Union."[1]

This is the core statement of the European Union for education and training. To develop and improve the education and training area the European Council has set up an action and development plan. This plan is called the Lisbon Strategy and was set in Lisbon, Portugal in 2000. Since it was created and the aims were adopted the political cooperation in education and training became stronger. As an effect of a stronger cooperation it was possible agreeing on common targets. New work programme and a strategic framework for European cooperation could be set up. "Education and Training 2010" or "ET 2020" are two of these work programmes to "encompass all types of education and training and all stages in lifelong learning."[2] Programmes as "Lifelong Learning Program" (2007-2013) or Erasmus Mundus (2009-2013) are only two of the funding supporter. But also agencies, other Initiatives and a number of networks are supporting the actions in education and training. One of these initiatives e.g. is the Central European Initiative (CEI). By following the same goals as the programmes and action plans of the European Union the most important aim is to make Europe one strong single market and "the most competitive and dynamic

[1] Cf. www.europa.eu; Education, training, youth, sport.
[2] Cf. www.europa.eu; Education and training – General Framework.

knowledge-based economy in the world capable of sustainable economic growth with more and better jobs and greater social cohesion."[3] Regardless to projects launched by the European Union to improve the general situation in the project area it is the most important to ensure a quality and sustainable education. Without education and training it is impossible to develop plans to improve and reduce the problems within the project area. Getting to know the general situation but also the specific needs of an area also belongs to a kind of learning and general education. Without this information it is also impossible to launch projects as the Central European Programme. Therefore it must be ensured that the education stays the most important part of developing Europe.

[3] Cf. Lisbon Strategy 2000; Employment, Economic Reform and Social Cohesion

The Lisbon Strategy

The Agenda of this meeting builds the basement for all further decisions taken about the education and training including the Life-long Learning Program which emerged from the Lisbon Process. The purpose of the meeting was to strengthen the economy and implement some long-term measures to make Europe the most competitive economic area in the world. It was required to take action because the world is influenced by an increasing globalization which makes it necessary to set the pace in all economic areas looking at the aim of becoming the strongest economy. The increase of Information and Communication Technology is accelerating and is of high importance for a life-long learning in private or professional way. Prior to the Lisbon Process other meetings as the Cardiff-, Cologne-, and Luxemburg Agenda have been taken place and set a range of instruments and processes so it was not necessary to create new and it was decided to strengthen and improve the existing ones. As already mentioned the rapid technological change was defining one of the most important areas of action of the Lisbon Process and setting a key factor in accessibility. Aim was to make ICT (Information and Communication Technology) available for as many people as possible. The system would not want to leave anyone behind doesn´t matter which social category, race, religion or gender. By shifting to knowledge driven society the European Union needs to adjust to a more global world by setting policy directions and cooperation with all member states. The level of education plays an important role in this connected world and can be improved by creating networks among education and training institutions. As a result of a higher educational level the European Union becomes more competitive and a real entrepreneurship can develop. The Council of Lisbon is not setting up only action plans for growth and development in an economic way but also considering sustainable macroeconomic stability, promoting social integration, ensuring support for a knowledge society and also guaranteeing social stability in times of an ageing population.[4]

The next chapter will give an introduction to the Bologna Process and its contents.

The Bologna Process

Within the Bologna Process the cooperation between countries in the European Union should be increased. As the main concept of the Process it encourages countries to reform their higher education system without taking the responsibility from the nations or universities neither taking away cultural or linguistic diversity. The cooperation shell be increased by implementing a more transparent system which is comparable to other countries´. The first step of reaching a more transparent higher education system is to equalize the diploma supplement to Bachelor – Master – Doctorate. Therefore the whole education is set with two cycles; a first one oriented to the labour market and a second one in condition to the complete the first. Also the recognition of the lectures within the cycles has to be adapted to an equal standard. In use here is the ECTS (European Credit Transfer System) which is also used for the Erasmus program. In terms of quality education the Bologna Process aims at an increase of cooperation between the HEIs (Higher Education Institutions) and to promote mobility for students, teachers and researchers.[5] The key competences for set-

[4] Cf. www.europa.eu; The Lisbon Special Council March 2000.
[5] Cf. www.europa.eu; The Bologna Process.

ting a basement for educational development are highlighted in the following paragraph.

The Key competences

The Lisbon Strategy makes it clear that the society is shifting to a knowledge-driven economy. The pace of change is rapid and accelerating and makes it urgent to act now to harness the full benefits of the opportunities presented.[6] Therefore the European Union in cooperation with the European Council set a range of key competences within the "Education and Training 2010 work program". Relating to the Lisbon agenda the focus point for growth and jobs is the area of education and training. The goal of setting up these key competences is to ensure that the member states are following the same direction and trying to reach similar long-term targets.[7]

After the economic downturn it is even more important to act effective and sustainable. Increasing pressure in public and private budget, loss of existing jobs and changing requirements for new jobs make it obligatory for education and training to be more open and respond to the needs of the people. Making the population better skilled for any upcoming challenges by being capable to deal with rapidly appearing changes, lead to the creation of a "knowledge-triangle". Therefore Hungary expanded their investments in Research & Development between 2008 and 2009 by 12% up to 299.388.032 million Hungarian Forint (around 1.109.345,13 Euros). At the same time the number of employees

---

[6] Cf. Lisbon Strategy 2000; Employment, Economic Reform and Social Cohesion
[7] Cf. www.europa.eu; key competences for a changing world (2010)

was raising in this period of time regardless the employment of researchers, technical employees or supporting staff.[8]

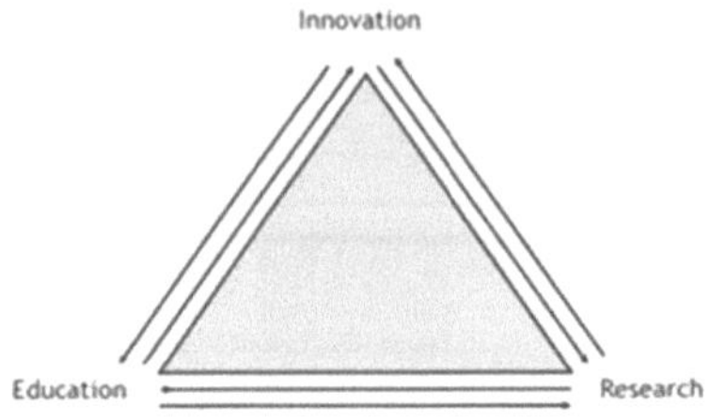

Figure 1: Knowledge Triangle

Although the Council endorsed a Strategic Framework for European Cooperation in Education and Training (ET 2009) it is still in responsibility of the member states to design their education system. With support of policy cooperation at European level it was possible to provide valuable support to countries´ educational reforms. In 2006 the Council for the first time set up a number of key competences. In the following three years these competences were implemented and benchmarking the Europeans average performance. The most important task about setting up indicators like the key competences is to evolve and emend lifelong learning strategies and any kind of education and training. The schooling has to be more specialized and relating to needs of the labour market, especially the vocational education and training (VET). Another problem is created by the downturn of the economy and the ignorance of how to respond

[8] Cf. www.statinfo.ksh.hu; Total R&D expenditure by financial sources.

on this alteration of requirements. "The progress in implementing a competence based approach, and the modernization of VET and higher education are key to Europe´s"[9] success.

As already mentioned the European Council set the so called key competences first in December 2006. They have been identical through the years. These are defined as eight competences to ensure "personal fulfilment, active citizenship, social inclusion and employability in a knowledge society."[10] The key competences are:

- Communication in the mother tongue
- Communication in foreign languages
- Mathematical competence and basic competence in science and technology
- Digital competence
- Learning to learn
- Social and civic competences
- Sense of initiative and entrepreneurship and
- Cultural awareness and expression

It is not a requirement to bring all of these qualities. The idea behind the key competences is to develop those with assistance of initial education and training to ensure everybody is set up and ready for working and learning. Exactly this initial education is one of the vital benchmarks just because the level of literacy has deteriorated within the last years. Most of the targets set for 2010 have not been reached what underlines a pending reform. The reform has started and already made quality progress although there is still much to do. Some of the member states use the key competences as a "reference point" to support

[9] Cf. www.europa.eu; key competences for a changing world (2010)
[10] Cf. Official Journal of the EU; Key competences for lifelong learning (2006)

teachers´ competence development or update assessment methods but also to introduce new ways of organization for curricula. Some of the key competences are becoming more prominent and, thus, deserve more attention for developing. Relating to the basic problems in literacy the competences to highlight are identified and benchmarked all the time. Fields such as mathematics or science but also mother tongue and foreign languages are taken under closer look to deteriorate these deficits considerably. Since the PISA survey in 2006 many action plans for raising the basic skills in reading, maths and science have been launched.[11]

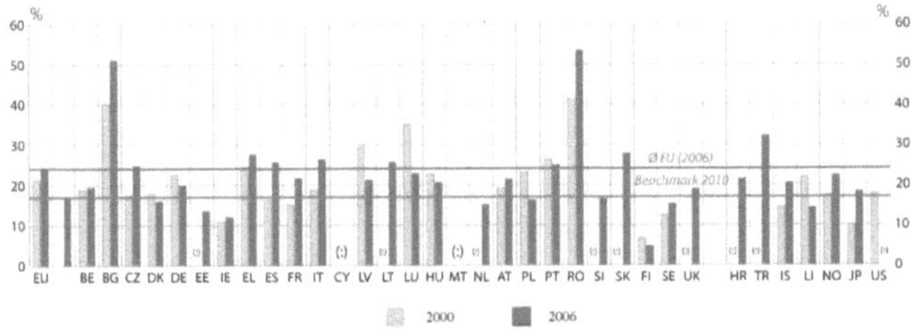

Figure 2: Pisa reading literacy scale[12]

Schools have to be taken more into responsibility to prepare pupils for further learning than only teaching them those skills and procure basic knowledge. Learning to learn is surely the elemental skill to develop.

Rising attention must also be paid to the Information and Communication Technology (ICT). In times of globalization and networking computing skills become more important. These competences belong to those who are rising out of the change to a knowledge-based economy. Schools and other education facilities

[11] Cf. Official Journal of the EU; Key competences for lifelong learning (2010)

[12] Cf. Official Journal of the EU; Delivering lifelong learning for knowledge, creativity and innovation (2008)

are in responsibility to adapt and embed these upcoming requirements into curricula. And again it is not only the sheer skills to be taught but also a critical thinking using new technologies as much as risk awareness and ethical and legal considerations.

Unfortunately many obstacles in developing new action plans and especially in implementing those plans can be found. The economic downturn is to mention as one of the external influences. It puts more pressure on to any area and as already mentioned it tightens up the private and public budget. But also fiscal policy or individual or demographic reasons can be found. Teacher mostly don´t have many incentives to improve their teaching. Most of the teachers prefer more professional development. Having a look on the demographic side shows debasement thru migration or in general people with disadvantaged background. They often have big gaps in basic education as reading, writing or math's and science. Different ways in dealing with these problems can be seen among the member states. Some are clearly trying to include fringe groups with deficits into the education system while others going for a segregated solution. Within the European Union the number of people with special needs of education has a wide range between 0,01% and 5,5% among overall student numbers in compulsory education.[13]

[13] Cf. Official Journal of the EU; Key competences for lifelong learning (2010)

% with low reading skills	All		Girls	Boys
	2000	2006	2006	2006
Germany	22,6	20	14,2	25,5
Hungary	22,7	20,6	13,2	27,3

Table 1: Pisa survey, low reading skills[14]

As seen in the table the number of people with low reading skills is still too high, even the numbers are decreasing it takes more afford to reach an acceptable level. Countries as Hungary show constantly decreasing numbers of pupils since 2005 in initial education but also the number of teachers is steadily decreasing since 2005.[15] These are further problems to fight against increasing problems in the field of education and training.

In most of the countries special programmes emerge to avoid pupils falling behind by an early acquisition of basic skills.

While it is naturally teaching basic skills in schools and other education facilities the VET is more focused on competences than on general education. Nevertheless it becomes more important through the evolving labour market and societal needs. This means that the key competences are taking a bigger part of the curricula also for adult training and their trainer and teachers. Relating on VET participation in Hungary the numbers are rising between the period of 2005 to

[14] Cf. Official Journal of the EU; Delivering lifelong learning for knowledge, creativity and innovation (2008)

[15] Cf. www.statinfo.ksh.hu; Main data on initial education.

2009 (162.030 up to 168.704). Unfortunately the numbers of people passing any VET exams is shrinking in the same period from around 40% to 30%.[16]

Programs as the “Life-long Learning Program” or Erasmus Mundus, launched by the European Union, are aiming to improve the educational and vocational training situation in Europe to reach an overall standardised level. Further information about these programs is following in the next chapters.

[16] Cf. www.statinfo.ksh.hu; Vocational education training.

2.2 Life-long learning Program 2007-2013

The life-long learning program is a program established by the European Union in 2006 after the decision No 1720/2006/EC from the European Parliament and is running from 2007-2013. 31 countries are participating in this program which aims for transnational learning mobility and to modernize education systems with cooperation projects.[17] It comprises all programs from the European Union regarding life-long learning. Former programs are Socrates, Leonardo da Vinci, eLearning and Jean Monnet Program. All of these programs were running from 2000-2006. Now the programs are summed in a single project to reach higher transparency and visibility in cooperation. It simplifies and increases every interaction by having one coherent strategy.[18] Since the adoption of the Lisbon Strategy in 2000 the focus is put more and more on education and growth, this program shell help to achieve the objectives also looking at the area for higher education decided in the Bologna Process. Already in the first three years of the program transnational education projects as well as training activities in 31 countries have been financed by using 3 billion Euros.[19] The society is shifting to a knowledge-driven economy and the most valuable assets are a high-quality education and training system including a life-long learning plan. Such a plan is formulated and the idea is to provide personal development for everybody as well as integration but also to participate in this knowledge economy. Goal number one in this plan is to facilitate a successful transition of the community exactly to this knowledge-driven society to reach sustainable development and a greater cohesion. The initial strategies and decisions were taken

[17] Cf. Life-long Learning Activity Report (2010).
[18] Cf. www.europa.eu
[19] Cf. Life-long Learning Activity Report (2010).

in 2000 within the Lisbon European Council. The European Union should become the most competitive and dynamic economy in the world. Therefore it is important to target week areas, develop strategies and promote sustainable growth from the beginning. Regarding to the EU legislation objectives of the LLP 2007-2013 are aimed to reduce borders for free movement of people, goods, services and money. Some other objectives are:

- Increasing attractiveness and accessibility for LLP opportunities
- Promoting creativity, competitiveness and employability
- Support ICT development and
- Reinforce a thinking of European citizenship by relating on mutual values (e.g. tolerance, respect)

Although the focus is put on becoming the strongest economic region there are also other aims for the program. Within following the main goal attention is also constantly put on reaching equality between men and women. There are still huge differences in the treatment and payment of men and women, reducing these differences is another side-goal of the project. Other problems showing up are xenophobia or racism as well as prejudices. All these problems need to be combated. With a project budget of 6,970 billion Euros the Life-long Learning Program is able to support and facilitate international and national but also regional and local projects.[20] Coming back to the structure of the LLP program it is divided into six sectorial sub-programs to ensure, that people at all age and education level can take part and improve their own skills. [21]

The **Comenius** program builds the first part of the LLP by focusing on preschool and school education up to the higher secondary school level. Addressing pupils, teachers, public authorities, educational staff, universities, parents´

[20] Cf. EACEA – Life-long Learning Program; Katia de Sousa (Florence, 2009).

[21] Cf. www.pnoconsultants.com

organizations but also teacher training institutes definitely shows the relevance for everybody in the education community. Objectives are clearly defined by "developing understanding and appreciation among young people and educational staff of the diversity of European cultures"[22] and "helping young people acquire the basic life-skills and competences necessary for their personal development, for future employment and for active European citizenship."[23] Other priorities are:

Motivation for learning and learning-to-learn skills

- Key competences: improving language learning; greater literacy; making science more attractive; supporting entrepreneurship; and reinforcing creativity and innovation
- Digital educational content and services
- School management
- Addressing socio-economic disadvantages and reducing early school leaving
- Participation in sports
- Teaching diverse groups of pupils
- Early and pre-primary learning

Children and pupils at very young age should get awareness for the importance of learning foreign languages or using and learning about ICT as a basic knowledge in a rapidly changing world. The constantly changing requirements make it also very important to ensure and develop teacher training and the pedagogical abilities of teachers or trainers. One ubiquitous point is the mobility. Also in the Comenius program pupil exchanges or staffs exchanges from

[22] Cf. www.europa.eu
[23] Cf. www.europa.eu

school to school a big topic to exchange experience and create new courses, curricula and general solutions. Especially for linking and promoting partnerships and school mobility 80% of the Comenius budget is planned. Within the former project circle 2000-2005 the budget amounted around 339.983.000 EUR.[24] The number of applications for funding is increasing yearly. The biggest increase can be seen in the area of In-Service Training (ICT). Rising from 15.500 up to 20.400 is showing an increase of 31%.[25]

The second part of the LLP is **Erasmus**, the former Leonardo da Vinci programme for higher education and vocational training. After the initial launch in 1987 it is now the best-known program addressing higher education on tertiary level. Purpose and objectives of the Erasmus is pursuing for innovations. "Erasmus centralized actions support transnational cooperation among higher education institutions and other relevant stakeholders across Europe through multilateral projects, including projects designed to reach out to the world of business, as well as networks and accompanying measures."[26] As already mentioned the total program budget for the LLP is 6,970 billion Euros. Around 40% of this budget is allocated to the Erasmus Program which means an amount of approximately 2,788 billion Euros. This program reaches up to 80% of the budget spending on mobility of students, teachers or other higher educational staff. Within the project duration the program shell encourage the mobility up to a number of 3 million individuals until 2012 as well as promoting the interaction between higher education institutions.[27] Last numbers by mid of 2010 were already showing a student mobility of 2.2 million individuals. Numbers are showing a constant increase in student mobility since the establishment of the Eras-

[24] Cf. www.europa.eu; A higher quality for schools; IP/05/1372; Brussels (2005).
[25] Cf. Life-long Learning Activity Report (2010).
[26] Cf. www.eacea.ec.europa.eu
[27] Cf. Official Journal of the EU; Decision No 1720/2006/EC; Article 21 (2006).

mus Program in 1987/88. From an initial number of 3244 students travelling in the first year up to 177.705 students in 2009/10 only on study reasons not regarding any placements abroad the program seems to be a total success. Taking a closer look at Hungary there is also a steady increase of outgoing Erasmus students (856 in 1998/99 up to 3421 in 2009/10).[28]

Country of the home institution	Lifelong Learning Programme - Erasmus								
	Study mobility 2007/08	Placement mobility 2007/08	Study + placement 2007/08	Study mobility 2008/09	Placement mobility 2008/09	Study + placement 2008/09	Study mobility 2009/10	Placement mobility 2009/10	Study + placement 2009/10
BE - België/Belgique/Belgien	4.781	605	5.386	5.041	904	5.945	5.269	1.078	6.347
BG - Balgarija	1.078	62	1.140	1.283	137	1.420	1.451	236	1.687
CZ - Česká republika	5.335	252	5.587	5.440	605	6.045	5.338	637	5.975
DK - Danmark	1.674	322	1.996	1.648	475	2.123	1.794	622	2.416
DE - Deutschland	23.553	2.733	26.286	23.407	4.487	27.894	24.029	4.825	28.854
EE - Eesti	595	122	717	551	207	758	725	214	939
GR - Ellas	2.308	160	2.468	2.737	292	3.029	2.790	389	3.179
ES - España	23.107	1.877	24.984	24.399	3.006	27.405	27.448	3.710	31.158
FR - France	22.556	3.389	25.945	23.560	4.723	28.283	24.426	5.787	30.213
IE - Éire / Ireland	1.514	303	1.817	1.421	415	1.836	1.600	528	2.128
IT - Italia	17.562	802	18.364	17.754	1.622	19.376	19.118	1.921	21.039
CY - Kypros	148	4	152	144	13	157	199	17	216
LV - Latvija	968	219	1.187	1.104	358	1.462	1.269	467	1.736
LT - Lietuva	2.392	261	2.653	2.425	575	3.000	2.277	725	3.002
LU - Lëtzebuerg/Luxembourg	367	5	372	426	0	426	445	23	468
HU - Magyarország	3.292	460	3.752	3.518	539	4.057	3.421	719	4.140
MT - Malta	107	10	117	142	9	151	122	67	189
NL - Nederland	4.699	1.287	5.986	4.902	2.103	7.005	5.358	2.320	7.678
AT - Österreich	4.133	475	4.608	4.053	886	4.939	4.234	878	5.112
PL - Polska	11.879	975	12.854	11.784	1.618	13.402	11.613	2.408	14.021
PT - Portugal	4.471	282	4.753	4.834	560	5.394	4.677	711	5.388
RO - Romania	2.953	426	3.379	3.064	680	3.744	3.129	865	3.994
SI - Slovenija	1.018	174	1.192	1.132	176	1.308	1.118	250	1.368
SK - Slovenská republika	1.452	245	1.697	1.703	317	2.020	1.798	353	2.151
FI - Suomi / Finland	3.265	687	3.952	3.436	975	4.411	3.529	1.020	4.549
SE - Sverige	2.348	193	2.541	2.413	270	2.683	2.728	269	2.997
UK - United Kingdom	7.523	2.756	10.278	7.429	3.397	10.826	8.053	3.670	11.723
IS - Island	210	6	216	186	12	198	215	10	225
LI - Liechtenstein	30	15	45	20	2	22	19	6	25
NO - Norge	1.103	51	1.154	1.317	93	1.410	1.262	94	1.356
TR - Türkiye	6.274	845	7.119	6.920	874	7.794	8.016	742	8.758
HR - Hrvatska							235	0	235
Total	162.695	20.002	182.697	168.193	30.330	198.523	177.705	35.561	213.266

Table 2: Outgoing Erasmus Students Under the Life-long Learning Program 2007/08 2009/10[29]

The table above shows the number of outgoing students within the duration of the Life-long Learning Program. The numbers are generally increasing since the establishment in 2007. Therefore it is possible to say that the implementation has a positive effect on the student mobility. Regarding to the numbers of the

[28] Cf. www.ec.europa.eu; Erasmus Statistics – Outgoing Students (2010).
[29] Cf. www.ec.europa.eu

LLP (Life-long Learning Program) the progress in integrating new member states e.g. Hungary is successful. The student mobility in Hungary is increasing through the project duration.

Also in this program the promotion of mobility among students and teaching staff increases the exchange of skills. The cultural understanding is growing and the awareness of cultural diversities as well as the respect and tolerance for different nationalities and cultures. As part of the Erasmus program the implementation of the ECTS system was set up within 1988 and 1995. This European Credit Transfer System (ECTS) should improve the transparency and the recognition of courses after returning to the home university. As a big advance of having one coherent system it makes performances comparable and ensures recognition at the home university was well as open the way to flexible learning paths. For a proper implementation of the system countries have to ensure a consistent use of the ECTS at all HEIs (Higher Education Institutes). The system not only makes performances comparable but also measures afford. The idea is that a student should have working hours of 1500 to 1800 a year. An envisaged average working load of 1600 hours p.a. (40 hours at 40 weeks) equals an annual amount of 60 ECTS. The working load does not only include the time in the University but also the preparation of the lectures at home and must therefore be based on the students afford and not on the time for teaching. Keeping the lectures up to date not only regarding the content but also relating on workload for the students regular evaluations are necessary and essential. Further requirements are to issue information about the courses in English and on beforehand the course starts. Also every student has to create and deliver a learning agreement which ensures the recognition of academic units between the exchanging universities. Basically the system has to ensure access to higher education and to make it as wide as possible.

Different than the Erasmus Program the **Leonardo da Vinci Programme** promotes vocational and educational training. Within this training the program also focuses on improving the attractiveness, the level of performance and vocational systems but also the transparency of structures and processes. Therefore the main actions in this program are transferring and developing innovation, networking and mobility and partnership. With an increasing mobility the possibilities for people to be trained and work abroad or generally in different places will rise. The whole program is aimed at increasing the knowledge and experience exchange in the professional area. In 2009 there have been 80.000 people receiving support from the Leonardo da Vinci Program for traineeship, apprenticeships or finding a job. The more people are travelling and working abroad the higher is the level of experience which is desirable for enterprises to become more competitive by gaining new skills.[30] As well as in the Erasmus program also in the Leonardo da Vinci program Germany and France are the two countries sending the most trainees with numbers of 15.800 and 7.200 people in 2009. For the Leonardo da Vinci program the budget for mobility and partnership accounts for at least 60%.[31]

The **Grundtvig Programme** is established especially for adults to improve in several ways. It is not limited to vocational or educational training but also improves job prospects through promoting personal development. The program was initiated in 2000 and is targeted at adults who never finished school because of leaving early and also foreign people who migrated and never had any opportunity to visit school. Through the demographic change the population is becoming older which means that there must be opportunities for older people. Exactly this group is facilitated in the Grundtvig Program. As well as in other

[30] Cf. www.ec.europa.eu
[31] Cf. www.europa.eu

programs of the life-long learning the main targets are networking in multilateral projects and increasing mobility. 55% of the budget of the Grundtvig program is therefore taken to support the mobility and partnership.

The next program doesn´t stop at sectoral borders. It was implemented to connect two or more programs to increase European cooperation. The transversal program also aims at increasing the transparency and quality level of education and training in Europe by targeting at policy co-operation with other countries relating to the Lisbon process 'Education and Training 2010' but also the Bologna and Copenhagen process, languages improvement and linguistic diversity, developing and promoting ICT (Information and Communication Technology) and an effective dissemination and exploitation of project results on a wide scale.[32]

The Jean Monnet Program builds the last of the six program areas of the Life-long Learning Program. The European Commission promotes a variety of university projects to create teaching skills for European integration. The project mainly supports projects and development in particular in Law, Economics, Political Science and History assuming that these are the key areas of increasing importance.

The Figure below shows the allocation of the funding of the Life-long Learning Program.

[32] Cf. www.pnoconsultants.com

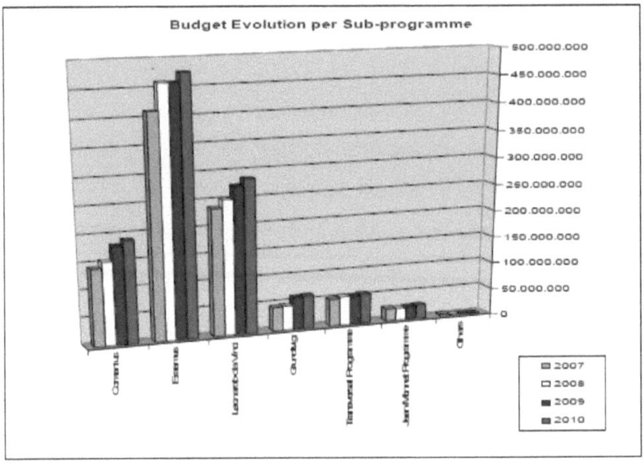

Figure 3: Budget Evolution per Sub-program[33]

The figure shows the allocation of the Life-long Learning Program budget and an Erasmus program absorbing most of the money by taking around 50%. Referring to the constant rise of funding for the Erasmus program it is clearly set, that the most important factor, for reaching the overall goal to become the strongest economic area in the world, is the cooperation and knowledge exchange with partners and other countries. Through the Erasmus Program also new member states are integrated in knowledge transfer and the increasing cooperation. Another advance and endeavour of the European Union is the improvement of language skills and cultural awareness and cultural enrichment.

After pointing out problems within the education system through tests as the PISA study focus has more set on several programmes to improve the education and training situation. As numbers and tables above show, situations are improving and developing towards a sustainable and problems-reduced future.

[33] Cf. Life-long Learning Activity Report (2010).

Programmes such as the Leonardo da Vinci or Erasmus count steadily rising numbers of participants and interested people. Many indicators show a real development e.g. in implementing the ECTS system or higher numbers of student mobility. Many problems still exist. Especially in the eastern countries of the European Union who are not yet as connected to western standards as other areas. Nevertheless programmes and plans are also set for these parts and even a wide range of action plans is already set the European Union is encouraged to ensure an ongoing improvement of all strategies. Since the implementation of projects numbers of set indicators are almost everywhere improving and it seems that further positive changes are only a matter of time.

3 CENTRAL EUROPE – Cooperation for Success

3.1 Introduction

Aiming to achieve an overall standard in Europe the European Territorial Co-operation 2007-2013 pushes economic and environmental development as well as social development in Central Europe. The CENTRAL EUROPE program is part of this policy framework and supports cooperation the between regions in the European Union.

The elaboration of joint solutions and the preparation of investments infrastructure in the fields of Innovation, Accessibility, Environment and Competitiveness and Attractiveness of Cities and Regions is focus point of this program. With a program budget of around 231 million Euros, funded by the European Regional Development Fund (ERDF), it is possible to support projects involving cooperation between national, regional and local actors in the period of 2007-2013.[34]

[34] Cf. European Territorial Cooperation; Recruitment Package

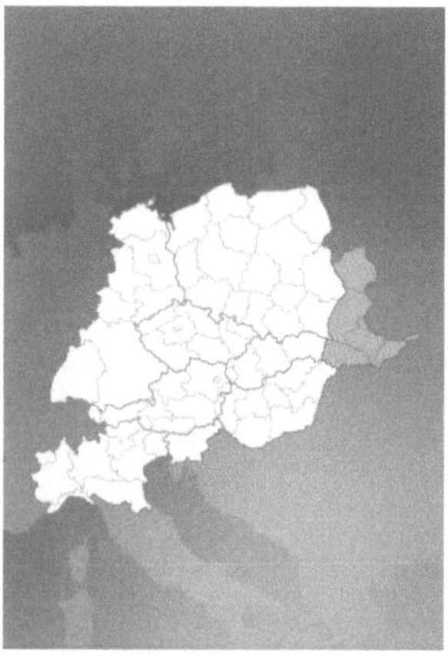

Figure 4: CENTRAL EUROPE Program Area[35]

Especially in this program regions like Austria, Czech Republic, Germany, Hungary, Italy, Poland and the Slovak Republic of Slovenia are served. Within the program countries are able to promote trans-national cooperation projects with mutual benefits, tangible outputs and concrete results while contributing to an integrated development of the entire program area to reduce these differences through cooperation.

Therefore the program has to play a considerable role in strengthening the development of these countries and their regions. This program elaboration aims to promote participation of special target groups like universities, development agencies, regional, local and national authorities, innovation centres and private actors in fields of innovation, economic development, as well as infrastructure and environment.

[35] Cf. www.eufa-wien.at

How does the Program work?

"CENTRAL EUROPE invites national, regional and local actors from the public and private sector to propose projects and apply for program funds. Following these calls, the submitted project proposals will be assessed. CENTRAL EUROPE Member State representatives will select the projects that, based on the quality of the submitted documentation, promise to deliver the best results. Project partners can be co-financed up to 85 percent, depending on their country of origin and on whether they are engaged in an economic activity or not. Partners will have to match the project budget with some of their own funds. Projects can have a total budget ranging of € 1-5 million. In exceptional cases, smaller or larger projects can also be funded."[36]

Central Europe at a Glance

The program covers about 1,050,000 square kilometres, an area that represents approximately a fifth of the EU landmass. About 148 million citizens or 28 percent of the EU population live in this area which means one of the biggest population mass potentials in Europe.[37] A huge variety of cultures, languages and ethnic groups can be found in this Central Europe Program area. There are more than twelve languages spoken and more than five languages of national and ethnic minorities, e.g. Romanes, Croatian or Ruthenian. Not only the variety of the people is big, but also the topography. Within the Program Area there are huge differences regarding climatic conditions, land use, settlement, accessibil-

[36] Cf. www.eufa-wien.at

[37] Cf. Central Europe; Operational Programme (2007).

ity, development processes or economic structures and ecological problems, as well as political and administrative structures, which are among the most heterogeneous in the European Union.

By using this great economic diversity as a strategic key factor, growth and territorial cohesion can be developed and strengthened. Summing up it is clear that the main characteristic and the challenge is to reduce economic and social disparities by "intensifying integration, reaching harmonized efficiency and quality standards, deepening existing and growing institutional networks, as well as cooperation and capacity building."[38]

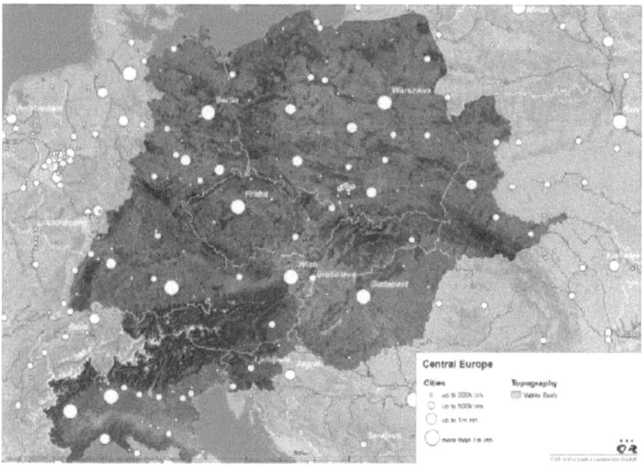

Figure 5: Landscape and settlement structures, 2007[39]

This figure shows the population density and the topographic variety the different areas are dealing with. The landscape is determined by the topography of

[38] Cf. Central Europe; Operational Programme (2007).
[39] Cf. www.epp.eurostat.ec.europa.eu

mountains, the sea, important river systems and a variety of border situations. Further important variables are the population density in these areas. Some parts of the Program Area have very low population density, e.g. Hungary, which is a quite rural country. The highest population density inside Hungary can be found in Budapest, the capital city, with about 1.72 million inhabitants in 2010 that was constantly decreasing with 2.01 million in 1990.[40]

Population and Demography

There is not only the already mentioned great diversity in topographic situations through the whole CENTRAL EUROPE Program Area. Also there are huge differences in demographic, social and cultural aspects. Demographic trends vary from a high increase in the number of population to a slight increase or stable population numbers in Germany until a slight decrease or major decrease in population numbers in Ukraine.[41] One reason for a decreasing population is the emigration to other countries. By opening the borders and making Europe one big economic area many young people are moving to the centre of Europe, away from the peripheral areas. This trend leads to a phenomenon called "brain drain" which makes it hard for the peripheral areas to maintain the current infrastructure. Follow ups of this trend are,

- low income level
- unfavourable housing conditions
- lower educational level and
- high unemployment rate

[40] Cf. www. portal.ksh.hu
[41] Cf. Central Europe; Operational Programme (2007); Page 13.

As a consequence social tensions rise and the circle start over with an increasing emigration rate. The population number is not only changing due to migration and emigration, but also due to decrease of birth-rates and increase of death rates. All these influences are leading to an ageing population without positive long term perspectives. The old-age-dependency ratio is expected to rise until 2030. This means that the average age of the population in these affected countries will become higher.[42] Especially the social- and health system is going to be under pressure by being challenged to keep up the level of support.[43] One more time the result of these negative trends is a decrease of population.

Despite to other regions the CENTRAL EUROPE Program area shows a huge number of different **social** and ethnic minorities. These groups in specific can be used to make a big step towards integrating other peripheral groups. They can be seen as a link between heterogeneous peoples. "Speaking their own language, organizing their specific cultural life and running educational and cultural institutions"[44] they are highly qualified to help intensifying the integration process. During this process of integration other programs are running to ensure the saving of the cultural heritage. Every folk has own customs and traditions to save and pass on to next generations. This can be material and immaterial cultural assets. Historical monuments and buildings are material assets and are protected and covered in a legislative framework (e.g. UNESCO). Immaterial assets are passed down from generation to generation and are usually valid only among one community.[45] Same as the population numbers and birth-rates also the cultural heritage is endangered and close to degrading big parts

[42] Cf. www.populationeurope.org, European Demographic Data Sheet 2006.
[43] Cf. Central Europe; Operational Programme (2008); Page 13.
[44] Cf. Central Europe; Operational Programme (2007); Page 13.
[45] Cf. UNESCO.

because of seeing the Program Area as one whole area instead of individual parts.

Economic Development and Labour Market

Not only the topography and the culture differ in the Program Area, also are there economic performance differences between the states. Following factors are mainly responsible for those:

- Market disparities concerning GDP, personal income, productivity, wage and many more. Highly developed countries vs. new Member States, rural vs. urban regions and accession countries.
- Technological progress during the integration process. Structural change and formation of new market structures.
- "Divergent accessibility to markets, labour and qualification, technology and innovation, transport and telecommunications networks, as well as to education and research."[46]
- Different economic activities and specialization for services and production as well as innovation potential (economic and enterprise structures, production costs and productivity)
- FDI (Foreign Direct Investments).[47]

Within Central Europe there are some of the richest but also some of the poorest regions. Relating to GDP numbers the range between the member states is still wide. Comparing some regions i.e. Wien, Austria with a GDP of 140% of EU-25 average to Chernovtsy, Ukraine with a GDP of 15% of EU-25 average it is impossible to reach an equal standard within the limited program

[46] Cf. Central Europe; Operational Programme (2007); Page 14.
[47] Cf. Central Europe; Operational Programme (2007); Page 14.

time until 2013.[48] Also countries as Hungary are showing constant increase of unemployment numbers since 2007 (7,4% to 11,2%).[49]

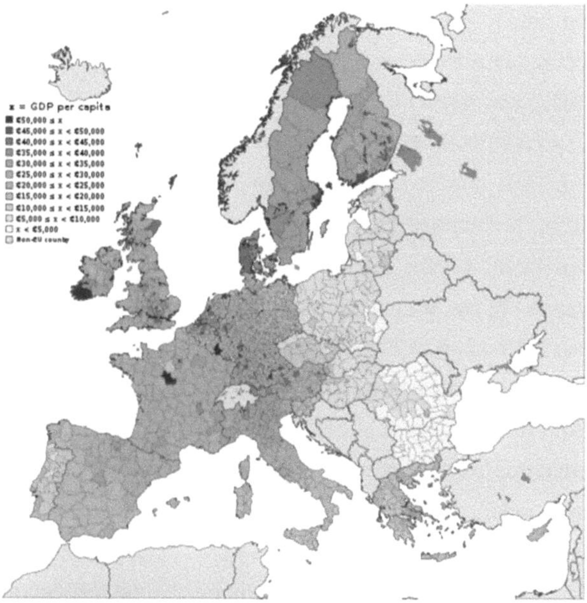

Figure 6: GDP per Capita 2007 (NUTS3)[50]

Furthermore 22 of 73 NUTS2 regions are lower than 50% of the EU-25 GDP average at which these are all upon the new member states. Usually the old member states are more competitive and more developed than new member states or neighbouring countries. Economically strong areas in the new member states are mostly the urban areas whereas the rural regions are far behind any

[48] Cf. Central Europe; Operational Programme (2007); Page 14.
[49] Cf. www.eurostat.eu
[50] Cf. www.epp.eurostat.ec.europa.eu

European average. Exactly these urbanized regions are showing dynamic growth rates relating to GDP numbers and it seems like they are catching up slowly. This situation is giving an outstanding position to the capital and mostly advanced regions of the new member states. Although trade relations are increasing and eastern countries are becoming trade partners of western countries the FDI is still equally important to community support. The FDI value still reaches between 20% and 40% of the total investment in Central Europe. These investments advantage one region but at the same time also disadvantage another by helping to increase the economic- and income disparities. All these influences have impact on the employment and unemployment situation in the specific regions. While some countries like Germany, Austria or Czech Republic can keep a standard of EU-25 level other countries are considerably lower. These countries are fighting against missing new job possibilities after a crises or increasing unemployment in the group of handicapped people, people with lower education or lower mobility. Taking the example of Hungary, people with higher mobility tend to leave the country searching for better labour market opportunities. The number of emigrating people from Hungary rose constantly since 1990.[51] On the other side, the general number of employed women, the number of people employed in the service sector and commuting networks are growing.

[51] Cf. www.epp.eurostat.ec.europa.eu

Accessibility

The field of accessibility, regarding transport, is of huge importance to the development and increase of the cross border trade. Unfortunately the accessibility varies widely still among the member states and the neighbouring countries. Highly developed countries as well as wide gaps in quality can be found. Especially the new member states often show weak accessibility in peripheral and rural areas. On top of these problems most of the countries put their focus on different means of transport. All countries increase their road transport whilst the railways are slightly decreasing in general.[52] Supported by the Trans-European Transport Network (TEN-T) the connection and inter European accessibility improves. Five major transport axes have been named to start the network for European transportation. Therefore a North-South and West-East connection has been strengthened as can be seen in the figure below.

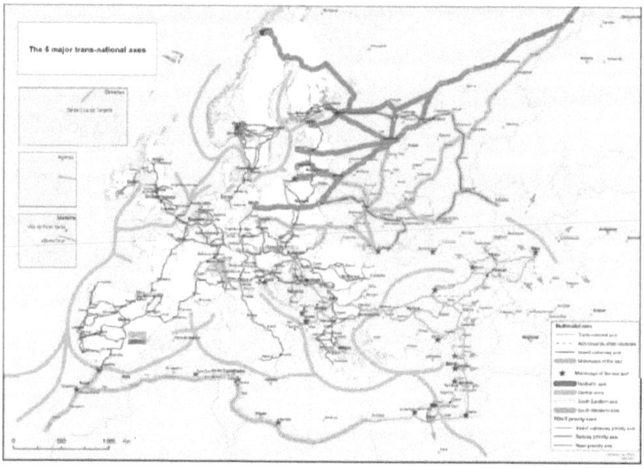

[52] Cf. Central Europe; Operational Programme (2007), Page 23.

Figure 7: 5 major trans-European transport axes[53]

The developing transport network realizes benefits in the logistics section. The increasing globalization makes it more important to have well developed railway, road or shipping and air transport networks. Whilst the road transport network is catching up to old member states average the waterway shipping is only utilizes by 10%.[54] Also the air transport is catching up with the "no-frills-airlines". As already mentioned the national and regional transport networks are mostly weak in the new member states (esp. eastern Hungary) and constrains around the capital cities. Usually they are oriented on economic centres. The transport infrastructure is more than unfavourable and reduces every kind of opportunity for cooperation. High-speed trains only exist in Germany. Clearly there is a need for a convenient, quick, flexible and ubiquitous public transport in a lot of new member states. Urban road networks are less densely developed and the level of car ownership is still lower in those countries. These countries also show a higher use of public transports, apparently because of the limited road space and the lower level of car ownership.[55]

Not only the transports but also the ICT (Information and Communication Technology) is part of the accessibility aspects. The development of the ICT in the new member states also shows differences. While the infrastructure in metropolitan areas is well developed, sparsely populated areas still show limited availability and restrictions regarding local disadvantages, low income due to unemployment or illness.[56] Whereas younger generations are educated in new technologies in school there is still a lack of education for the elderly population.

---

[53] Cf. Central Europe; Operational Programme (2007); Maps, Page 138.
[54] Cf. Central Europe; Operational Programme (2007); Page 24.
[55] CF. www.transportbenchmarks.eu, Urban Transport Initiative, Year two (2005).
[56] Cf. Central Europe; Operational Programme (2007); Page 26.

But also the internet- use of enterprises is lagging behind (especially Hungary). In general the new member states are not on an equal level as the EU-15 states. Some areas are catching up faster, others slower and some are stagnating without any progress.

The following chapter will show strategies and goals of the CENTRAL EUROPE PROGRAM 2007-2013.

3.2 Goals and Direction

The CENTRAL EUROPE PROGRAM 2007-2013 is not only about following one goal, neither about territorial cohesion, nor about integration and not only about enhancing competitiveness. The program aims for a complete cover of all these targets. Following the Lisbon agenda for growth, competitiveness and employment as well as the Gothenburg guideline for sustainability the goal for the program is for the EU to become the most competitive economy in the world by "strengthening territorial cohesion, promoting internal integration and enhancing the competitiveness of Central Europe."[57]

Through increasing mobility and developing the transport network it becomes more likely that disadvantages of more rural and peripheral areas will decrease. Reaching territorial cohesion firstly means to not exclude people because of where they live. It has to be first priority to get fair access to services and general interest for everybody irrespective of the area they happen to live. Prerequisite for territorial cohesion is the integration in a social, economic and territorial way. Barriers and obstacles have to be removed in order to ensure accessibility and free movement for everybody. Therefore regulations have to be har-

[57] Cf. Central Europe; Operational Programme (2007); Page 36.

monized, common standards have to be set and networks have to be optimized. Integrating Central Europe means to integrate a lot of potential and diversity in a social, ecological and cultural dimension. Also in this area the great diversity is seen as a key strategic factor for development to make Europe the strongest economy in the world. Competitiveness cannot be reached only by trying to improve pure economic performance. It is more a combination of territorial cohesion, internal integration and competitiveness. A sustainable and strong economy can only be reached by improving innovation and ensuring access to information systems and efficient transport systems to optimize territorial structures.[58]

Therefore the Program has two defined strategies to pursue these goals.

- Improving competitiveness of Central Europe by strengthening innovation and accessibility structures and
- Improving territorial development in a balanced and sustainable way by enhancing the quality of the environment and developing attractive cities and regions.[59]

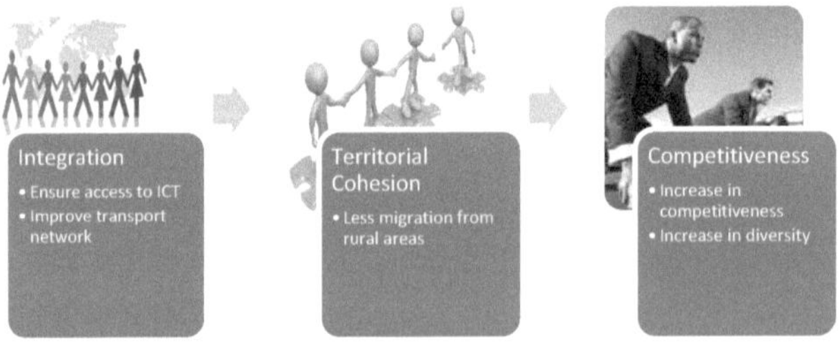

[58] Cf. Territorial Agenda of the European Union; Page 2; Leipzig (May 2007).
[59] Cf. Central Europe; Operational Programme (2007); Page 38.

Ensuring accessibility to Information and Communication Technology and improving the transport networks in rural, peripheral and sparsely populated areas leads to a higher territorial cohesion. No access and no perspective for the future is the main issue in peripheral areas. By increasing the territorial cohesion and providing access people have fewer reasons to migrate to metropolitan areas and can find work at home. Follow ups of this progress line is an increase of the competitiveness and diversity. Exactly this increase in diversity is the key factor to use the potential in all regions leading to a strong knowledge-based economy.[60]

The strategies are followed through different priorities whereas the development of innovation, accessibility, environmental responsibility and enhancing competitiveness and attractiveness of cities and regions are focused on.

Developing innovation is surely one of the most important tasks by concentrating on strengths and addressing to specific needs to reduce the weaknesses. To improve accessibility means to use the created innovations and fully observe a sustainable development to strengthen Central Europe. Whilst sensitizing for environmental responsibility by promoting sustainable approaches to "natural resource management, risk reduction and the enhancement of the natural environment"[61] enhancing the competitiveness by developing cities and regions is the last of the four priorities of the program.

Following these priorities it is important to reach sustainable progress at any time. This means an environmentally friendly use of resources to not limit or reduce future development possibilities. Sustainability can only be reached through covering every dimension. Therefore affords have to be spread over an

[60] Cf. Jahrbuch der Europäischen Integration; Page 159 (2010).

[61] Cf. Central Europe; Operational Programme (2007); Objective Tree Central Europe.

ecological, economical and social dimension. Aim of the program is not to reach the minimum level set, but to reach the highest possible standard to ensure a sustainable use of natural resources.

At the same time existing processes and structures are reviewed and improved. Especially in the field of ICT there is a lot of research and development to find new approaches.

The following chapters will take a closer look at the four priorities of the Central Europe Program strategies.

CENTRAL EUROPE Precedence´s

As shown before, the conditions across the member states vary widely. Many countries have to deal with unfavourable situations and are far from reaching European standards or catching up with other highly developed countries. Innovation is the most important opportunity to a competitive and successful economy. It also brings the ability of flexibility. Innovation helps every region to use their potential for development and growth. The migration to more urban and metropolitan areas can be reduced by bringing future potential back to rural and peripheral regions. Especially the younger and well educated part of the population is causing the brain-drain by moving to capital cities. Therefore the rural and sparsely populated areas have to be integrated better and provided with sufficient access to ICT.

The first step to improve innovation is to enhance the framework conditions through a transnational cooperation. Enhancing mutual learning, capacity building and know-how transfer are the main aims. Therefore the program has set a range of activities by

- ensuring that all key players are searching for innovative approaches and policies for implementing an exchange and coordination system (e.g. through foresight initiatives)
- "supporting and establishment and development of transnational clusters in key competence areas"[62]
- networking between public authorities and financial institutions to increase the capability in financial engineering

---

[62] Cf. Central Europe; Operational Programme (2007); Page 61.

- interfering between public and private players
- establishing facilities for technology transfer in a supranational dimension and
- supporting the R&TD institutions and easy accessibility[63]

Whilst metropolitan areas are widely connected to every kind of ICT or R&TD systems, peripheral regions are not. Exactly this lack of access is often the problem for missing development in the particular area. Not everybody has the same chances and possibilities to access these technologies. Within an implementation of capabilities to spread and apply innovation these disparities should be reduced for a higher exploitation of research results. The diffusion of innovation and building up networks on the other side improves the cooperation between key players to bring the knowledge also to disadvantaged regions. After setting up rural areas with a network of ICT the next step is to improve those networks to transnational networks to foster transnational and transregional communication.[64] Although a well developed network will increase the accessibility to technologies and integrate regions it is by far not enough. To avoid future gaps it is necessary to start solving problems from their origin. The education and training is therefore put into focus since one of the aims of the CEP is to transfer the society into a knowledge-based economy. Cooperation at all levels is essential whether for educational, training or research institutions but also linking the academic and business sector to reach a transnational cooperation. Creating working and action plans for human resource and knowledge devel-

[63] Cf. Central Europe; Operational Programme (2007); Page 61.
[64] Cf. Central Europe; Operational Programme (2007); Page 62.

opment but also to reduce migration and brain-drain and reach a demographic change.[65]

For many times now, the accessibility has been mentioned as one of the most important factors in integrating rural and sparsely populated regions. It can also be seen as a necessary precondition with strong relation to territorial cohesion. As part of the program the aim is not only to develop accessibility and establish a network of technology and transport systems but also to ensure that every region is improving on the same level. Disparities in the development are to be avoided strictly. Whilst the TEN-T is helping to increase the mobility it is exactly this mobility and offer of new possibilities making regions more attractive for innovative investments and opportunities for new services. Within the area of improving accessibility within Central Europe on part is to improve the interconnectivity. Searching for transnational solutions the aim is to find a way to address specific needs for every region (urban, rural, metropolitan, remote and isolated areas). Integrating also the isolated regions makes it necessary to think of intermodal transport solutions and develop a strategic cooperation within trans-European transport corridors. This variety of transportation also helps to reduce bottlenecks, which are rising through the increasing mobility and traffic, especially road traffic. Fostering an establishment for cooperation between all parties is necessary to ensure sustainable, the specific needs meeting, environmentally friendly development of accessibility.

Another aspect of improving accessibility is to make transports safe. Through the increasing mobility and the higher traffic volumes public urban transports are facing problems like increasing need for maintenance and rising financial budget. The number of people commuting is increasing. Following approaches

[65] Cf. Central Europe; Operational Programme (2007); Page 63.

to develop novel technological solutions shell ensure a sustainable solution for the future. These technological approaches are not only researching in the area of how to make mobility safe but also developing the ICT to make it less necessary of physical mobility. Using ICT for video-conferencing or supply-chain-management are two possibilities to reduce this need and help the environment to regenerate.[66]

Within the next chapter these issues dealing with the use of resources to achieve a sustainable and responsible environment are shown and solutions presented.

Any kind of progress and development needs to include responsible thinking in order to not exploit the resources for the current success and also to ensure that current actions are not jeopardizing the possibilities for the future. Every possibility of growth is showing opportunities but also threats for the environment. Talking about the environment itself means to talk about responsibilities in three areas an ecological, an economical and last but not least a social dimension. Protecting and treating all three dimensions with responsibility is essential and a pre-condition for sustainable growth. Target groups on different levels and interest groups are set. National, regional and local bodies, mainly from the field of environment, are targeted but also management groups working in the field of water, risk or natural resources are involved. On the other side research institutions, associations or SME´s can be found to increase the efficiency of using natural resources, milder the effect of man-made threats for the environment or foster research for developing environmentally friendly technologies. Therefore in 2006 the European Council established a renewed SDS (Sustainable Development Strategy). Based on the Gothenburg strategy from

[66] Cf. Central Europe; Operational Programme (2007); Page 69.

2001 and reviewed since 2004 the efficient use of resources by focusing on renewable energies is essential for ensuring a healthy and permanently regenerating environment. At the same time the use of raw materials should be decreased to reduce the impact on the nature. Through an efficient use of resources and developing eco-efficient innovations advantages in competition can be realized. Former approaches can also be found in the INTERREG programs for a "socio-economic development without damaging ecological functions."[67] In the CENTRAL EUROPE PROGRAM there are also strategies and risk-management plans developed on a transnational level to deal with any man-made hazards rising out of the integration of the new member states and especially the rural and peripheral areas. Aside these development of risk plans and similar strategies, the main strategy to avoid hazards and achieve a healthy environment is to foster renewable energy sources as well as putting afford in a higher efficiency of energy use. Following aims to reduce the use of fossil energy resources the Kyoto protocol can be fulfilled and help to reduce CO2 emissions. In order to ensure equal possibilities for the future economy reducing the fossil energy use is a big step forward reaching a sustainable and attractive environment.[68]

The balance of achieving a healthy environment and a sustainable and competitive economy is to spread activity. Especially in the new member states there are mostly strong metropolitan capital regions showing economical competitiveness. This mono-centric structure is partly the reason for the migration and the rise of disparities between metropolitan areas and peripheral regions. Spreading the economical activities and using the natural resources from the

[67] Cf. Central Europe; Operational Programme (2007); Page 70.
[68] Cf. Central Europe; Operational Programme (2007): Page 75.

smaller regions will develop a polycentric structure and decrease disparities. Also the numerous medium size towns carry a lot of economic potential but cannot develop because of missing infrastructure and accessibility. Rise the attractiveness of cities and regions will bring a chance for economic prosperity. As a follow up to this polycentric strategy a balanced territorial development is the aim. Making cities more attractive does not mean to simply increase the economic performance and aim at a financial thinking, but also in terms of a demographic change and an ageing population it is becoming more important to adjust the living circumstances. Services and, above all, the housing situation have to be adjusted to the social trend. On the other side using the cultural heritage of cities or regions can be used and capitalized against all economic pressure to destroy and give space for investments. In this way regions keep their identities and attractiveness.[69]

Financial Distribution

The European Union firstly established the European Regional Development Fund in 1975 to support least prosperous regions in the EU. After the number of members of the EU grew, the ERDF developed into a strong instrument to help equalizing regional imbalances and is jointly funded by the European Union. Lead partners or project partners can apply for a funding of this ERDF. The maximum funding differs between the regions. Whilst countries like Hungary, Poland, Slovakia, Slovenia and Czech Republic are eligible of 85% other countries including Germany, Austria or Italy can only get 75% of their projects funded. Financial support for projects is only related to the four priorities already

[69] Cf. Central Europe; Operational Programme (2007); Page 78-80.

mentioned above. The budget volume of the ERDF amounts to EUR 246.011.074 and is part of the overall program budget of EUR 298.295.837.[70] A breakdown of the annual funding can be seen in the table below.

1 **Year**	2 **ERDF**
2007	34,211,355
2008	32,982,238
2009	33,560,339
2010	34,677,260
2011	35,825,424
2012	36,851,074
2013	37,903,384
Total 2007-2013	**246,011,074**

Table 3: Year by source for the program (in EUR)[71]

Another detailed structure for utilization of the funding can be seen in next table.

[70] Cf. www.eurofundingnw.org

[71] Cf. Central Europe; Operational Programme (2007); Page 87.

EUR	A	B	Indicative breakdown of the national counterpart		E=A+B	F=A/E	For Information	
	Community Funding	National counterpart B=C+D	C National public funding	D National private funding	Total funding	Co-financing rate	EIB-contribution	Other funding
Priority axis 1: Facilitating innovation across Central Europe	49,202,215	10,077,562	9,372,133	705,429	59,279,777	0.83	0	0
Priority axis 2: Improving accessibility of and with Central Europe	63,962,879	13,100,831	12,707,806	393,025	77,063,710	0.83	0	0
Priority axis 3: Using our environment responsibly	63,962,879	13,100,831	12,707,806	393,025	77,063,710	0.83	0	0
Priority axis 4: Enhancing competitiveness and attractiveness of cities and regions	54,122,437	11,085,318	10,752,758	332,560	65,207,755	0.83	0	0
Priority axis 5: Technical assistance	14,760,664	4,920,221	4,920,221	0	19,680,885	0.75	0	0
Total	**246,011,074**	**52,284,763**	**50,460,724**	**1,824,039**	**298,295,837**		0	0

Table 4: Priority axes by source of funding.[72]

In this table there is another fifth priority included. The technical assistance includes activities like evaluation, information, management and monitoring. Another part is to ensure the administrative capacities for implementing the funds as well as control activities. The support is meant for projects planned and running within the eight member states of the Central Europe area. The usual budget of one to five million Euros can vary in exceptions upwards or downwards. It is also possible that projects are supported which are not part of the Central Europe region but have positive results on this region. Since the establishment the Program approved 96 projects between March 2008 and December 2010.[73]

One of these is the SoNorA project for higher accessibility and interconnectivity.

[72] Cf. Central Europe; Operational Programme (2007); Page 88.
[73] Cf. www.central2013.eu

3.3 SoNorA – South North Axis

The SoNorA Project started in November 2008 and is running for 40 month until February 2012. The lead partner is the Veneto region in Italy but in total there are 25 partners in 9 EU countries involved as well as 35 associated institutions. The overall project budget amounts to 7.098.964,99 million Euros whereas 5.551.180,84 million Euros are funded by the European Research and Development Fund.[74]

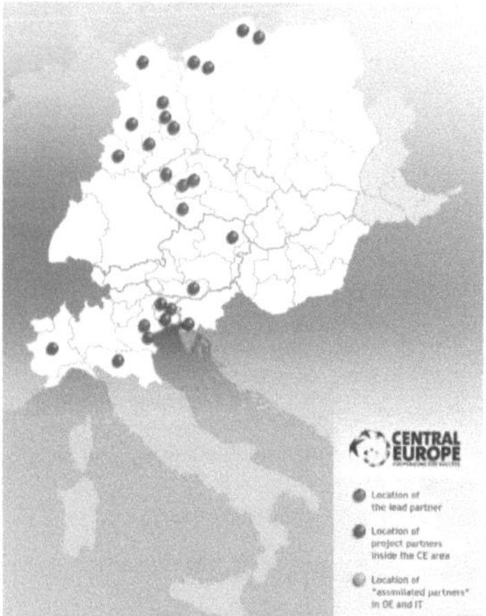

Figure 8: SOuth-NORth-Axis Project partner map[75]

One of the aims of the project is to promote regional development and as already mentioned the projects priority is to reach a higher accessibility within the

[74] Cf. www.sonoraproject.eu
[75] Cf. www.central2013.eu; SoNorA Project.

South-North-Axis by developing a real network and promoting primary transport infrastructure. Focusing on the region between the Adriatic and Baltic Seas the objectives are clearly set. Reducing obstacles in infrastructure realization to implement freight logistic services is one of them as well as to assist in regional development through network improvements. In addition to these objectives specific aims are the facilitation of combined traffic solutions (i.e. waterways, road and railroad) and the improvement of accessibility of enclosed countries, especially the promotion of individual regions with a trans-national relevance. Follow ups of an increased accessibility and improved multimodal transport network are a positive impact on the social and territorial cohesion as well as on integration. The development of an intermodal transport network also has positive impact on the environment by increasing the use of railroad transportation instead of road transportation as the most important way. Along with social cohesion and integration comes an increase of competitiveness through development of professional and academic trans-national networks and knowledge and expertise exchange. Among the project also the already existing TEN-T network will be renewed and plans for inland waterway transportations are taken into consideration. Further to an extension of the intermodality measures for analyzing investment impacts on nodes and network links are developed.

The whole project is structured in six Working Packages (WP) whereas three of them (WP3, WP4 and WP5) have technical functions. Every Work Package has its own responsible body. The Lead Partner is in charge for the first WP to guarantee a strong, solid and trouble-free management. The Veneto region as the Lead Partner is also responsible for cooperation with the management bodies. The second WP is lead by the Association of Chambers of Commerce of the Veneto Region. They ensure a high participation and a wide knowledge by generating attention through dissemination of objectives and results. This approach is not limited to a national level but also includes a transnational distribution. Whereas the third WP, under control by the Czech Railways, is focusing on optimised networks the fourth WP is concentrating on attaining the network infrastructure. The Marshal's Office of Zachodniopomorskie Voivodeship ensures this through surveys about forlorn issues, pre-investment studies for key links and international interventions for promoting trouble-free allocation of technical parameters and scheduling of infrastructure. Similar to the former WP Luka Koper as responsible port % logistics system is searching for relevant service solutions and developing business plans as well as sectorial logistic services in WP fife. Another permanent action is the rework of ICT software to arrange bottlenecks. The German Association for Housing, Urban & Spatial Development provides a communication platform for SoNorA partners and associated institutions. Therefore the sixth WP is reviewing key results.[76]

[76] Cf. www.sonoraproject.eu

Results and Perspective

Through the different means of transport a variety of service and support systems have been developed which have to be set on standard ISO levels to ensure cooperation. Adjusting the systems is important for interconnectivity and simplification of multimodal transport systems. The primary transport system so far has been the road and railway but within this project waterways are presented as real alternatives. Waterway transportation is a relatively safe mode of transport given the safety measures that vessel builders must comply with while building their ships and it is an environmentally friendly mode of transport. Within the Sonora project another piloted approach is running in Austria which also aims on promoting inland waterway transportation on the Danube. This project is funded with one million Euro per anno and an extra 18€ - 34€ for every container transport on waterways.[77] The basic financial support is used to provide international navigation on the Danube. After the period until 2014 the effects of the piloted programme can be measured and further project promotion for waterway transportation support can be decided.

[77] Cf. www.central2013.eu; Analysis of the inland waterway network in the Sonora project are (2010).

4 Conclusion and Outlook

The European Union takes huge afford and is anxious to reach an equal standard among all member states. As mentioned in the previous chapters this endeavour is realised through multiple programmes and projects in various fields. The promotion of one strong competitive economic area is the overall aim for all countries participating in any programmes. Some countries are already reaching policy recommendations set by the European Commission or National or Regional Authorities. Others have to improve and develop areas with deficits and guarantee sustainable catching up to stronger countries. This is reached through trans-national cooperation on all governmental levels and by help of partner associations. After highlighting the programs of the EU and revealing the structure and processes of the Central Europe Program one question is which positive impacts can be seen in the supported regions. "Are these countries catching up to European standards, or not". This question is about to be answered within a variety of fields. Mainly relating on the fields mentioned in the previous chapter the progress here will be determined through development of the areas higher education and training and changes in labour markets situation.

Firstly Considering the education and training sector the student numbers in Hungary are steadily falling in the period of 2007 until 2009. In total the number decreased by almost 5% since 2007 while the average of reducing student numbers in the 27 member states is around 0.3%.[78]

Not only the student numbers are regressing, also the employment rates in the group of 15-64 year-olds. Within the last four completed years the percentage of

[78] Cf. Appendix A5; Pupils and students.

employed people in Hungary lost 2%. With a total percentage of employed people of 55.4% in 2010 Hungary is still around 10% below EU average. In the same period Germany reached a slight increase of 0.5% up to 71.1% which is still 7% above EU average. Programs in the field of vocational and educational training could be responsible for the differences but as a matter of fact the unemployment numbers are constantly rising in Hungary since 2007. This development shows clearly a still existing lack of ability to create new job possibilities and re-employ or redeploy those people. 11.2% is by far the highest unemployment rate in Hungary within the last 15 years. After four years of establishing the Central Europe Program there are still huge disparities in infrastructure among the countries. This is emphasized through and reduction of unemployed of 1.6% in Germany since 2007.[79]

Searching for reasons to explain the negative trend in development of population numbers in countries as Hungary and other new member states a questionnaire has been created. The survey targeted mainly Hungarian students and with higher education to identify reasons for the emigration of your professionals leading to a lack of those in their home country.

In total 144 people have been asked mostly between the age of 21 and 26. The interviewees were all from Hungary and living in the Borsod-Abaúj-Zemplén region. 88% of them are students and studying at the University of Miskolc (Miskolci Egyetemvaros). As already mentioned Hungarian professionals are decreasing in the country through emigration. This trend can also be seen in the survey where 83% are planning to live abroad after graduation and only 17% are planning to come back whereas no one wanted to stay in the country after graduating. Relating on reasons, given in the poll, almost half of them is search-

[79] Cf. Appendix A4; A3; Unemployment rate & Employment rate.

ing for a new challenge abroad but 100% of is going for a better salary and social benefits. Summing up people are willing to leave the country immediately for money and social contribution but to make them come back it takes much more. Even though the level of social benefits and salary are developing positive in Hungary only 55 of the 144 interviewees would come back. Reaching a sustainable development by keeping young professionals in the country requires strong development of the whole infrastructure.

List of References and Sources

Central Europe 2013 Sonora programm.

Online available

http://www.central2013.eu/fileadmin/user_upload/Downloads/outputlib/SoNorA_O3.4.1_uploaded.pdf.

ERDF questions & answers.

Online available

http://www.eurofundingnw.org.uk/ERDF_questions.asp?section=fund#whatisERDF, zuletzt geprüft am 22.07.2011.

Home | EU-Funds-Navigator.

Online available

http://www.funds-navigator.eu/index.php/funds-navigator-mainmenu-532.html?task=detail&id=32, zuletzt geprüft am 25.07.2011.

KSH Statinfo.

Online available

http://statinfo.ksh.hu/Statinfo/haViewer.jsp, zuletzt geprüft am 29.07.2011.

Lifelong Learning Programme. Activity Report 2009 - 2010.

Online available

http://ec.europa.eu/education/lifelong-learning-programme/doc/activity0910_en.pdf.

Urban Transport Benchmarking Initiative (2007).

Online available http://www.transportbenchmarks.eu/publications/reports.html, zuletzt aktualisiert am 21.11.2007, zuletzt geprüft am 19.07.2011.

Delivering lifelong learning for knowledge, creativity and innovation (2009).

Online available http://europa.eu/legislation_summaries/education_training_youth/general_framework/ef0005_en.htm, zuletzt aktualisiert am 29.03.2011, zuletzt geprüft am 09.06.2011.

Lifelong Learning Programme 2007-13 (2009).

Online available http://europa.eu/legislation_summaries/education_training_youth/lifelong_learning/c11082_en.htm, zuletzt aktualisiert am 14.06.2011, zuletzt geprüft am 25.07.2011.

The Lisbon Special European Council (March 2000): Towards a Europe of Innovation and Knowledge (2009).

Online available http://europa.eu/legislation_summaries/education_training_youth/general_framework/c10241_en.htm, zuletzt aktualisiert am 14.06.2011, zuletzt geprüft am 27.07.2011.

Work programme on the follow-up of the objectives of education and training systems in Europe (2009).

Online available

http://europa.eu/legislation_summaries/education_training_youth/general_framework/c11086_en.htm, zuletzt aktualisiert am 29.03.2011, zuletzt geprüft am 11.05.2011.

EUROPA - Money and the EU (2010).

Online available

http://europa.eu/about-eu/basic-information/money/index_en.htm, zuletzt aktualisiert am 19.05.2011, zuletzt geprüft am 07.06.2011.

Key competences for a changing world (2010).

Online available

http://europa.eu/legislation_summaries/education_training_youth/general_framework/ef0020_en.htm, zuletzt aktualisiert am 29.03.2011, zuletzt geprüft am 08.06.2011.

The Bologna process: setting up the European Higher Education Area (2010).

Online available

http://europa.eu/legislation_summaries/education_training_youth/general_framework/c11088_en.htm, zuletzt aktualisiert am 14.06.2011, zuletzt geprüft am 27.07.2011.

Jean Monnet Program - About Us (2011).

Online available

http://centers.law.nyu.edu/jeanmonnet/intro.html, zuletzt aktualisiert am 03.02.2011, zuletzt geprüft am 26.07.2011.

LLP Lifelong Learning Programme (2011).

Online available

http://www.pnoconsultants.com/About-Grants/eu-grants/Pages/llp-lifelong-learning-programme.aspx, zuletzt aktualisiert am 25.07.2011, zuletzt geprüft am 25.07.2011.

SoNorA (2011).

Online available

http://www.sonoraproject.eu/, zuletzt aktualisiert am 28.07.2011, zuletzt geprüft am 28.07.2011.

07A1010; publisher; [Nachname nicht vorhanden] (2006): Lisbon European Council 23-24.03.2000: Conclusions of the Presidency. -.

Online available

http://www.europarl.europa.eu/summits/lis1_en.htm, zuletzt aktualisiert am 07.12.2006, zuletzt geprüft am 11.05.2011.

Appendix: A1: Eurostat - Tables, Graphs and Maps Interface (TGM) table.

Online available

http://epp.eurostat.ec.europa.eu/tgm/table.do?tab=table&init=1&language=de&pcode=tps00001&plugin=0, zuletzt geprüft am 31.07.2011.

Appendix: A2: Eurostat - Tables, Graphs and Maps Interface (TGM) table.

Online available

http://epp.eurostat.ec.europa.eu/tgm/table.do?tab=table&init=1&language=de&pcode=tps00003&plugin=0, zuletzt geprüft am 31.07.2011.

Appendix: A3: Eurostat - Tables, Graphs and Maps Interface (TGM) table.

Online available

http://epp.eurostat.ec.europa.eu/tgm/table.do?tab=table&init=1&language=de&pcode=tsiem010&tableSelection=1&plugin=0, zuletzt geprüft am 31.07.2011.

Appendix: A4: Eurostat - Tables, Graphs and Maps Interface (TGM) table.

Online available

http://epp.eurostat.ec.europa.eu/tgm/table.do?tab=table&plugin=0&language=de&pcode=tsiem110, zuletzt geprüft am 29.07.2011.

Appendix: A5: Eurostat - Tables, Graphs and Maps Interface (TGM) table.

Online available

http://epp.eurostat.ec.europa.eu/tgm/table.do?tab=table&init=1&language=de&pcode=tps00051&plugin=0, zuletzt geprüft am 31.07.2011.

COMM/EAC (2011): European Commission - Education & Training - lifelong learning programme - Leonardo da Vinci programme.

Online available

http://ec.europa.eu/education/lifelong-learning-programme/doc82_en.htm, zuletzt aktualisiert am 25.02.2011, zuletzt geprüft am 25.07.2011.

COMM/EAC (2011): European Commission - Education & Training - Erasmus - Statistics.

Online available

http://ec.europa.eu/education/erasmus/doc920_en.htm, zuletzt aktualisiert am 07.07.2011, zuletzt geprüft am 26.07.2011.

COMM/EACEA/R1 (2011): Lifelong learning - Erasmus | EACEA.

Online available

http://eacea.ec.europa.eu/llp/erasmus/erasmus_en.php, zuletzt aktualisiert am 25.07.2011, zuletzt geprüft am 25.07.2011.

COMM/PRESS/01 (2005): EUROPA - Press Releases - Comenius: Improving the quality of European schools and teachers.

Online available
http://europa.eu/rapid/pressReleasesAction.do?reference=IP/05/1372&format=HTML&aged=0&language=EN&guiLanguage=en, zuletzt aktualisiert am 04.11.2005, zuletzt geprüft am 31.07.2011.

COMM/TREN/A (2006): Directorate-general Energy and Transport - Figures and Main Facts.

Online available
http://ec.europa.eu/dgs/energy_transport/figures/trends_2030/index_en.htm, zuletzt aktualisiert am 01.08.2006, zuletzt geprüft am 19.07.2011.

COUNCIL OF European Union: Review of the EU Sustainable Development Strategy.

CREATOR (2010): European Commission - Environment - Sustainable Development.

Online available

http://ec.europa.eu/environment/eussd/, zuletzt aktualisiert am 27.07.2010, zuletzt geprüft am 21.07.2011.

Erdody, Michal; Webaholix; o, s. r.: central2013.eu - Information on the Application Process.

Online available

http://www.central2013.eu/central-projects/applying-for-a-project/information-on-the-application-process/, zuletzt geprüft am 22.07.2011.

Erdody, Michal; Webaholix; o, s. r. (2011): central2013.eu - Funded Projects.

Online available

http://www.central2013.eu/nc/central-projects/approved-projects/funded-projects/?tx_fundedprojects_pi1[project]=26, zuletzt aktualisiert am 28.07.2011, zuletzt geprüft am 28.07.2011.

Erwin Aligam - styleshout.com (2011): EUFA.

Online available

http://www.eufa-wien.at/ce_e_index.html, zuletzt aktualisiert am 06.07.2011, zuletzt geprüft am 08.07.2011.

European Commission (Hg.): Central Europe - Cooperation for Success. Oparational Programme.

Online available

http://www.central2013.eu/fileadmin/user_upload/Downloads/Document_Centre/Programme_Documents/OP_Central_Europe_approved EC__2007_12_03.pdf

.

Mr Riccardo Maratini: SOuth-NORth Axis. Central Europe 2013.

Online available

http://www.central2013.eu/nc/central-projects/approved-projects/funded-projects/?tx_fundedprojects_pi1[project]=26.

Werner Weidenfeld, Wolfgang Wessels (2011): Jahrbuch der Europäischen Integration. 2010. 1. Auflage 2011. Baden Baden.

Appendix

Index to Appendices

Appendix A1: Total Population

Appendix A2: Population density

Appendix A3: Employment rate, group 15-64

Appendix A4: Unemployment rate

Appendix A5: Pupils and students

Appendix A6: Crossing boarders for a strong united Europe

Appendix: A1

Total population

At 1 January

	2000	2001	2002	2003	2004	2005	2006	2007	2008	2009	2010	2011
European Union (27 countries)	482767512	483797028	484635119	486646114	488797929	491134938	493210397	495291925	497686229	499705496	501120688	502489143
Euro area (17 countries)	314097369	315413267	316972081	318909529	320931192	323030150	324813716	326560819	328487272	329991881	330931820	331965504
Euro area (16 countries)	312725298	314046308	315610839	317553484	319580123	321682640	323469032	325218410	327146337	328651466	329591693	330625310
Belgium	10239085	10263414	10309725	10355844	10396421	10445852	10511382	10584534	10666866	10753080	10839905	10918405
Bulgaria	8190876	8149468	7891095	7845841	7801273	7761049	7718750	7679290	7640238	7606551	7563710	7504868
Czech Republic	10278098	10266546	10206436	10203269	10211455	10220577	10251079	10287189	10381130	10467542	10506813	10532770
Denmark	5330020	5349212	5368354	5383507	5397640	5411405	5427459	5447084	5475791	5511451	5529449	5560628
Germany (including former GDR fron	82163475	82259540	82440309	82536680	82531671	82500849	82437995	82314906	82217837	82002356	81802257	81751602
Estonia	1372071	1366959	1361242	1356045	1351069	1347510	1344684	1342409	1340935	1340415	1340127	1340194
Ireland	3777565	3832783	3899702	3964191	4028851	4111672	4208156	4312526	4401335	4450030	4467854	4480176
Greece	10903757	10931206	10968708	11006377	11040650	. 11082751	11125179	11171740	11213785	11260402	11305118	11329618
Spain	40049708	40476723	40964244	41663702	42345342	43038035	43758250	44474631	45283259	45828172	45989016	46152926
France	60545022	60979315	61424036	61864088	62292241	62772870	63229635	63645065	64007290	64369147	64716310	65075310
Italy	56923524	56960692	56993742	57321070	57888245	58462375	58751711	59131287	59619290	60045068	60340328	60626442
Cyprus	690497	697549	705539	715137	730367	749175	766414	778684	789269	796875	803147	804435
Latvia	2381715	2364254	2345768	2331480	2319203	2306434	2294590	2281305	2270894	2261294	2248374	2229641
Lithuania	3512074	3486998	3475586	3462553	3445857	3425324	3403284	3384879	3366357	3349872	3329039	3244601
Luxembourg	433600	439000	444050	448300	454960	461230	469086	476187	483799	493500	502066	511840
Hungary	10221644	10200298	10174853	10142362	10116742	10097549	10076581	10066158	10045401	10030975	10014324	9986000
Malta	380201	391415	394641	397296	399867	402668	405006	407810	410290	413609	414372	417608
Netherlands	15863950	15987075	16105285	16192572	16258032	16305526	16334210	16357992	16405399	16485787	16574989	16654979
Austria	8002186	8020946	8063640	8100273	8142573	8201359	8254298	8282984	8318592	8355260	8375290	8404252
Poland	38653559	38253955	38242197	38218531	38190608	38173835	38157055	38125479	38115641	38135876	38167329	38200037
Portugal	10195014	10256658	10329340	10407465	10474685	10529255	10569592	10599095	10617575	10627250	10637713	10636979
Romania	22455485	22430457	21833483	21772774	21711252	21658528	21610213	21565119	21528627	21498616	21462186	21413815
Slovenia	1987755	1990094	1994026	1995033	1996433	1997590	2003358	2010377	2010269	2032362	2046976	2050189
Slovakia	5398657	5378783	5378951	5379161	5380053	5384822	5389180	5393637	5400998	5412254	5424925	5435273
Finland	5171302	5181115	5194901	5206295	5219732	5236611	5255580	5276955	5300484	5326314	5351427	5375276
Sweden	8861426	8882792	8909128	8940788	8975670	9011392	9047752	9113257	9182927	9256347	9340682	9415570
United Kingdom	58785246	58999781	59216138	59435480	59697037	60038695	60409918	60781346	61191951	61595091	62026962	62435709
Iceland	279049	283361	286575	288471	290570	293577	299891	307672	315459	319368	317630	318452
Liechtenstein	32426	32863	33525	33863	34294	34600	34905	35168	35356	35589	35894	36152
Norway	4478497	4503436	4524066	4552252	4577457	4606363	4640219	4681134	4737171	4799252	4858199	4920305
Switzerland	7164444	7204055	7255653	7313853	7364148	7415102	7459128	7508739	7593494	7701856	7785806	7866500
Montenegro	612496	614791	617085	619300	621258	622978	623576	624896	627508	630142	632922	:
Croatia	4497735	4438868	4444608	4442744	4441733	4443901	4442884	4441238	4436401	4435056	4425747	:
Former Yugoslav Republic of Macedo	2021578	2031112	2038651	2023654	2029892	2035196	2038514	2041941	2045177	2048619	2052722	2057284
Turkey	66889425	67895581	68838069	69770026	70692009	71610009	72519974	69689256	70586256	71517100	72561312	73722988

http://epp.eurostat.ec.europa.eu/tgm/table.do?tab=table&plugin=0&language=en&pcode=tps00001

Appendix: A2

Population density
Inhabitants per km²

	1998	1999	2000	2001	2002	2003	2004	2005	2006	2007	2008	2009
European Union (27 countries)	:	:	112,3	112,5	112,8	113,3	113,9	114,3	114,8	115,5	116	:
Belgium	336,4	336,8	338	339,2	340,7	342,1	343,6	345,5	347,8	350,4	353,1	356
Bulgaria	74,4	74	73,6	71,3	70,9	70,5	70,1	69,7	69,4	69	68,7	:
Czech Republic	133,2	133,1	132,9	132,4	132	132,1	132,2	132,5	132,9	133,8	135	:
Denmark	123,1	123,4	123,8	124,3	124,7	125,1	125,4	125,7	126,2	126,7	127,5	:
Germany (including former GDR from 1991)	229,7	230	230,2	230,6	231	231,2	231,1	230,9	230,7	230,4	229,9	:
Estonia	31,9	31,7	31,5	31,4	31,3	31,2	31,1	31	30,9	30,9	30,9	:
Ireland	54,2	54,8	55,4	56,1	57,3	58,4	59,5	60,8	62,3	63,7	64,7	65,2
Greece	82,9	83,3	83,5	83,8	84,1	84,3	84,6	84,9	85,2	85,6	85,9	:
Spain	78,5	78,9	79,6	80,5	81,6	83	84,4	85,8	87,2	89,4	90,8	:
France	94,9	95,4	96	96,7	97,4	98,1	98,8	99,6	100,2	100,9	101,4	:
Italy	192,8	192,9	193	193,1	193,7	195,2	197,1	198,6	199,7	201,2	202,7	204
Cyprus	73,4	74,2	75	75,8	76,8	78,1	80	81,9	83,5	84,8	85,7	86,5
Latvia	38,7	38,4	38,1	37,8	37,5	37,3	37,1	36,9	36,7	36,5	36,4	:
Lithuania	56,6	56,2	55,8	55,5	55,3	55,1	54,8	54,5	54,2	53,9	53,6	:
Luxembourg	164,2	166,5	168,7	170,7	172,5	174,6	177,1	179,9	182,8	185,6	189	192,5
Hungary	108,7	108,2	108,8	109,5	109,2	108,9	108,6	108,4	108,3	108,1	107,9	:
Malta	1196	1216	1235	1245	1255	1263	1272	1279	1281	1296	1304	:
Netherlands	463,6	466,7	470,2	473,7	476,7	480,3	481,9	483,1	483,8	485,3	487,2	:
Austria	96,7	:	97,2	:	98	98,5	:	99,8	:	:	101,1	:
Poland	123,6	123	122,4	122,3	122,3	122,2	122,1	122,1	122	121,9	121,9	:
Portugal	109,9	110,4	111	112	112,8	113,6	114,1	114,5	114,9	115,2	115,3	:
Romania	97,9	97,7	97,6	97,5	94,8	94,5	94,3	94,1	93,9	93,7	93,6	:
Slovenia	98,4	98,6	98,8	98,9	99,1	99,1	99,2	99,3	99,6	100,2	100,4	:
Slovakia	109,9	110	110,1	109,7	109,7	109,7	109,8	109,9	110	110,1	110,3	:
Finland	16,9	17	17	17	17,1	17,1	17,2	17,2	17,3	17,4	17,5	:
Sweden	21,5	21,6	21,6	21,7	21,8	21,8	21,9	22	22,1	22,3	22,5	:
United Kingdom	239,9	240,7	241,5	242,4	243,3	244,3	246,9	247,7	249,2	250,8	:	:
Iceland	2,7	2,8	2,8	2,8	2,9	2,9	2,9	3	3	3,1	3,2	:
Liechtenstein	200	200	206,3	206,3	212,5	212,5	212,5	217,2	219	220,4	221,7	:
Norway	14,4	14,5	14,7	14,7	14,8	14,9	15,1	15,2	15,3	15,5	15,6	:
Switzerland	177,8	178,6	179,5	180,7	182,3	183,5	183,5	185,9	187,1	188,8	191,2	:
Montenegro	:	:	:	:	:	:	:	:	:	:	:	:
Croatia	:	:	:	78,5	78,6	78,5	78,5	78,5	78,5	78,4	78,4	:
Former Yugoslav Republic of Macedonia, the	80,6	81	81,3	81,2	81,1	81,4	81,6	81,8	81,9	82	82,2	:
Turkey	84,7	86,2	87,6	88,8	90,1	91,3	92,5	93,6	93	:	92,3	:

http://epp.eurostat.ec.europa.eu/tgm/table.do?tab=table&init=1&language=en&pcode=tps00003&plugin=0

Appendix: A3

Employment rate, group 15-64
%
Total

	1996	1997	1998	1999	2000	2001	2002	2003	2004	2005	2006	2007	2008	2009	2010
European Union (27 countries)	:	60,7	61,2	61,8	62,2	62,6	62,4	62,6	63	63,5	64,5	65,4	65,9	64,6	64,2
European Union (25 countries)	:	60,6	61,2	61,9	62,4	62,8	62,8	63	63,4	64	64,8	65,8	66,3	65	64,5
European Union (15 countries)	60,3	60,7	61,4	62,5	63,4	64,1	64,2	64,5	64,9	65,4	66,2	66,9	67,3	65,9	65,4
Euro area (17 countries)	:	58,6	59,3	60,4	61,4	62,1	62,3	62,6	63,1	63,7	64,7	65,6	66	64,7	64,2
Euro area (16 countries)	:	58,5	59,3	60,4	61,4	62,1	62,3	62,6	63,1	63,7	64,7	65,6	66	64,7	64,2
Belgium	56,2	56,8	57,4	59,3	60,5	59,9	59,9	59,6	60,3	61,1	61	62	62,4	61,6	62
Bulgaria	:	:	:	:	50,4	49,7	50,6	52,5	54,2	55,8	58,6	61,7	64	62,6	59,7
Czech Republic	:	:	67,3	65,6	65	65	65,4	64,7	64,2	64,8	65,3	66,1	66,6	65,4	65
Denmark	73,8	74,9	75,1	76	76,3	76,2	75,9	75,1	75,7	75,9	77,4	77,1	77,9	75,7	73,4
Germany (including former GDI	64,1	63,7	63,9	65,2	65,6	65,8	65,4	65	65	66	67,5	69,4	70,7	70,9	71,1
Estonia	:	:	64,6	61,5	60,4	61	62	62,9	63	64,4	68,1	69,4	69,8	63,5	61
Ireland	55,4	57,6	60,6	63,3	65,2	65,8	65,5	65,5	66,3	67,6	68,7	69,2	67,6	61,8	60
Greece	55	55,1	56	55,9	56,5	56,3	57,5	58,7	59,4	60,1	61	61,4	61,9	61,2	59,6
Spain	47,9	49,5	51,3	53,8	56,3	57,8	58,5	59,8	61,1	63,3	64,8	65,6	64,3	59,8	58,6
France	59,5	59,6	60,2	60,9	62,1	62,8	63	64	63,8	63,7	63,7	64,3	64,9	64,1	64
Italy	51,2	51,3	51,9	52,7	53,7	54,8	55,5	56,1	57,6	57,6	58,4	58,7	58,7	57,5	56,9
Cyprus	:	:	:	:	65,7	67,8	68,6	69,2	68,9	68,5	69,6	71	70,9	69,9	69,7
Latvia	:	:	59,9	58,8	57,5	58,6	60,4	61,8	62,3	63,3	66,3	68,3	68,6	60,9	59,3
Lithuania	:	:	62,3	61,7	59,1	57,5	59,9	61,1	61,2	62,6	63,6	64,9	64,3	60,1	57,8
Luxembourg	59,2	59,9	60,5	61,7	62,7	63,1	63,4	62,2	62,5	63,6	63,6	64,2	63,4	65,2	65,2
Hungary	52,1	52,4	53,7	55,6	56,3	56,2	56,2	57	56,8	56,9	57,3	57,3	56,7	55,4	55,4
Malta	:	:	:	:	54,2	54,3	54,4	54,2	54	53,9	53,6	54,6	55,3	54,9	56
Netherlands	66,3	68,5	70,2	71,7	72,9	74,1	74,4	73,6	73,1	73,2	74,3	76	77,2	77	74,7
Austria	67,8	67,8	67,9	68,6	68,5	68,5	68,7	68,9	67,8	68,6	70,2	71,4	72,1	71,6	71,7
Poland	:	58,9	59	57,6	55	53,4	51,5	51,2	51,7	52,8	54,5	57	59,2	59,3	59,3
Portugal	64,1	65,7	66,8	67,4	68,4	69	68,8	68,1	67,8	67,5	67,9	67,8	68,2	66,3	65,6
Romania	:	65,4	64,2	63,2	63	62,4	57,6	57,6	57,7	57,6	58,8	58,8	59	58,6	58,8
Slovenia	61,6	62,6	62,9	62,2	62,8	63,8	63,4	62,6	65,3	66	66,6	67,8	68,6	67,5	66,2
Slovakia	:	:	60,6	58,1	56,8	56,8	56,8	57,7	57	57,7	59,4	60,7	62,3	60,2	58,8
Finland	62,4	63,3	64,6	66,4	67,2	68,1	68,1	67,7	67,6	68,4	69,3	70,3	71,1	68,7	68,1
Sweden	70,3	69,5	70,3	71,7	73	74	73,6	72,9	72,1	72,5	73,1	74,2	74,3	72,2	72,7
United Kingdom	69	69,9	70,5	71	71,2	71,4	71,4	71,5	71,7	71,7	71,6	71,5	71,5	69,9	69,5
Iceland	:	:	:	:	:	:	:	83,3	82,3	83,8	84,6	85,1	83,6	78,3	78,2
Liechtenstein	:	:	:	:	:	:	:	:	:	:	:	:	:	:	:
Norway	:	:	:	:	77,5	77,2	76,8	75,5	75,1	74,8	75,4	76,8	78	76,4	75,3
Switzerland	77	76,9	78	78,4	78,3	79,1	78,9	77,9	77,4	77,2	77,9	78,6	79,5	79	78,6
Montenegro	:	:	:	:	:	:	:	:	:	:	:	:	:	:	:
Croatia	:	:	:	:	:	:	53,4	53,4	54,7	55	55,6	57,1	57,8	56,6	54
Former Yugoslav Republic of Ma	:	:	:	:	:	:	:	:	:	:	39,6	40,7	41,9	43,3	43,5
Turkey	:	:	:	:	:	:	:	:	:	:	44,6	44,6	44,9	44,3	46,3
United States	72,9	73,5	73,8	73,9	74,1	73,1	71,9	71,2	71,2	71,5	72	71,8	70,9	67,6	66,7
Japan	69,5	70	69,5	68,9	68,9	68,8	68,2	68,4	68,7	69,3	70	70,7	70,7	70	70,1

http://epp.eurostat.ec.europa.eu/tgm/table.do?tab=table&init=1&language=en&pcode=tsiem010&tableSelection=1&plugin=0

Appendix: A4

Unemployment rate by gender

%

Total

	1993	1994	1995	1996	1997	1998	1999	2000	2001	2002	2003	2004	2005	2006	2007	2008	2009	2010
European Union (27 count	:	:	:	:	:	:	:	8,7	8,5	8,9	9	9,1	9	8,3	7,2	7,1	9	9,7
European Union (25 count	:	:	:	:	:	9,4	9,1	8,6	8,4	8,8	9	9,1	9,1	8,3	7,3	7,1	9,1	9,8
European Union (15 count	10	10,3	10	10,1	9,9	9,3	8,6	7,7	7,3	7,7	8	8,1	8,3	7,8	7,1	7,2	9,2	9,6
Euro area (17 countries)	:	:	10,4	10,6	10,6	10,1	9,4	8,5	8,1	8,5	8,9	9	9,2	8,5	7,6	7,6	9,6	10,1
Euro area (16 countries)	:	:	10,4	10,6	10,6	10,1	9,4	8,5	8,1	8,5	8,9	9	9,2	8,5	7,6	7,6	9,6	10,1
Belgium	8,6	9,8	9,7	9,5	9,2	9,3	8,5	6,9	6,6	7,5	8,2	8,4	8,5	8,3	7,5	7	7,9	8,3
Bulgaria	:	:	:	:	:	:	:	16,4	19,5	18,2	13,7	12,1	10,1	9	6,9	5,6	6,8	10,2
Czech Republic	:	:	:	:	:	6,4	8,6	8,7	8	7,3	7,8	8,3	7,9	7,2	5,3	4,4	6,7	7,3
Denmark	9,6	7,7	6,7	6,3	5,2	4,9	5,2	4,3	4,5	4,6	5,4	5,5	4,8	3,9	3,8	3,3	6	7,4
Germany (including forme	7,6	8,2	8	8,7	9,4	9,1	8,2	7,5	7,6	8,4	9,3	9,8	11,2	10,3	8,7	7,5	7,8	7,1
Estonia	:	:	:	:	:	:	:	13,6	12,6	10,3	10	9,7	7,9	5,9	4,7	5,5	13,8	16,9
Ireland	15,6	14,3	12,3	11,7	9,9	7,5	5,6	4,2	3,9	4,5	4,6	4,5	4,4	4,5	4,6	6,3	11,9	13,7
Greece	:	:	:	:	:	10,8	12	11,2	10,7	10,3	9,7	10,5	9,9	8,9	8,3	7,7	9,5	12,6
Spain	18,4	19,5	18,4	17,8	16,7	15	12,5	11,1	10,3	11,1	11,1	10,6	9,2	8,5	8,3	11,3	18	20,1
France	11	11,6	11	11,5	11,5	11	10,4	9	8,3	8,6	9	9,3	9,3	9,2	8,4	7,8	9,5	9,8
Italy	9,8	10,6	11,2	11,2	11,3	11,3	10,9	10,1	9,1	8,6	8,4	8	7,7	6,8	6,1	6,7	7,8	8,4
Cyprus	:	:	:	:	:	:	:	4,9	3,8	3,6	4,1	4,7	5,3	4,6	4	3,6	5,3	6,3
Latvia	:	:	:	:	:	14,3	14	13,7	12,9	12,2	10,5	10,4	8,9	6,8	6	7,5	17,1	18,7
Lithuania	:	:	:	:	:	13,2	13,7	16,4	16,5	13,5	12,5	11,4	8,3	5,6	4,3	5,8	13,7	17,8
Luxembourg	2,6	3,2	2,9	2,9	2,7	2,7	2,4	2,2	1,9	2,6	3,8	5	4,6	4,6	4,2	4,9	5,1	4,5
Hungary	:	:	:	9,6	9	8,4	6,9	6,4	5,7	5,8	5,9	6,1	7,2	7,5	7,4	7,8	10	11,2
Malta	:	:	:	:	:	:	:	6,7	7,6	7,5	7,6	7,4	7,2	7,1	6,4	5,9	7	6,9
Netherlands	5,5	6,2	7,1	6,4	5,5	4,3	3,5	3,1	2,5	3,1	4,2	5,1	5,3	4,4	3,6	3,1	3,7	4,5
Austria	:	3,8	3,9	4,3	4,4	4,5	3,9	3,6	3,6	4,2	4,3	4,9	5,2	4,8	4,4	3,8	4,8	4,4
Poland	:	:	:	:	10,9	10,2	13,4	16,1	18,3	20	19,7	19	17,8	13,9	9,6	7,1	8,2	9,6
Portugal	5,5	6,8	7,2	7,2	6,7	5,6	5	4,5	4,6	5,7	7,1	7,5	8,6	8,6	8,9	8,5	10,6	12
Romania	:	:	:	:	:	:	7,1	7,3	6,8	8,6	7	8,1	7,2	7,3	6,4	5,8	6,9	7,3
Slovenia	:	:	:	6,9	6,9	7,4	7,3	6,7	6,2	6,3	6,7	6,3	6,5	6	4,9	4,4	5,9	7,3
Slovakia	:	:	:	:	:	12,6	16,4	18,8	19,3	18,7	17,6	18,2	16,3	13,4	11,1	9,5	12	14,4
Finland	16,3	16,6	15,4	14,6	12,7	11,4	10,2	9,8	9,1	9,1	9	8,8	8,4	7,7	6,9	6,4	8,2	8,4
Sweden	9,1	9,4	8,8	9,6	9,9	8,2	6,7	5,6	5,8	6	6,6	7,4	7,7	7,1	6,1	6,2	8,3	8,4
United Kingdom	10,2	9,3	8,5	7,9	6,8	6,1	5,9	5,4	5	5,1	5	4,7	4,8	5,4	5,3	5,6	7,6	7,8
Iceland	:	:	:	:	:	:	:	:	:	:	:	:	:	:	:	:	:	:
Liechtenstein	:	:	:	:	:	:	:	:	:	:	:	:	:	:	:	:	:	:
Norway	6	5,4	4,9	4,7	3,9	3,1	3	3,2	3,4	3,7	4,2	4,3	4,5	3,4	2,5	2,5	3,1	3,5
Switzerland	:	:	:	:	:	:	:	:	:	:	:	:	:	:	:	:	:	:
Montenegro	:	:	:	:	:	:	:	:	:	:	:	:	:	:	:	:	:	:
Croatia	:	:	:	:	:	:	:	:	:	14,8	14,2	13,7	12,7	11,2	9,6	8,4	9,1	11,8
Former Yugoslav Republic	:	:	:	:	:	:	:	:	:	:	:	:	:	:	:	:	:	:
Turkey	:	:	:	:	:	:	:	:	:	:	:	:	9,2	8,7	8,8	9,7	12,5	10,7
United States	6,8	6,1	5,6	5,4	4,9	4,5	4,2	4	4,8	5,8	6	5,5	5,1	4,6	4,6	5,8	9,3	9,6
Japan	2,5	2,9	3,1	3,4	3,4	4,1	4,7	4,7	5	5,4	5,3	4,7	4,4	4,1	3,9	4	5,1	5,1

http://epp.eurostat.ec.europa.eu/tgm/table.do?tab=table&init=1&language=en&pcode=tsiem110&tableSelection=1&plugin=0

Appendix: A5

Pupils and students

Excluding pre-primary education (1 000)

	1998	1999	2000	2001	2002	2003	2004	2005	2006	2007	2008	2009
European Union (27 countries)	94285	95787	95840	96023	97266	97027	97893	98318	93901	93247	93113	92958
Belgium	:	2206,8	2234,8	2303,5	2332,6	2373	2333	2380,2	2409,5	2417,7	2427,7	2436
Bulgaria	1403,9	1389,5	1357,1	1322	1274,9	1273,9	1250,1	1225,7	1192,5	1175,2	1141,8	1110,5
Czech Republic	1913,9	1875,2	1906,2	1931,8	1935,3	1927,7	1933,7	1911,9	1869,3	1855,6	1855,4	1849,1
Denmark	972,7	988,3	1003	1029,4	1046	1069,4	1127,3	1144,2	1141,8	1154,5	1151,6	1159,7
Germany (including former GDR from	14568	14581	14549	14515	14511	14525	14583	14467	14394	14251	14065	13984
Estonia	289,9	295,5	302,9	305,9	304	298,4	292,9	288,6	278,3	268,4	257,5	250
Ireland	1000	994,1	990,1	986,8	992,2	1000,8	1032,7	1037,2	1035,7	1054,3	1053,4	1076,4
Greece	1904,3	1858,8	1883,5	1905,7	1975,3	1960,7	1982,9	2052,6	2042	1964,4	2008,7	:
Spain	8086,8	7898,3	7768,6	7597,3	7461,2	7381,6	7509,2	7537	7529,2	7555,7	7615,3	7677,1
France	12092	12022	11934	11849	11791	11884	11903	12315	12321	12296	12265	12251
Italy	9202,3	9151,1	9049,2	9143,6	9198,7	9266,2	9380	9408,9	9464,4	9500,2	9510,4	9513,5
Cyprus	:	138,1	138	139,6	141,5	145,9	148,1	146,6	146	145,8	148,4	152,3
Latvia	470,6	484,6	498,6	509,7	510,1	505,8	501,8	491	472,4	449,8	430,6	413,6
Lithuania	713	739,1	766,8	787,3	796,6	806,8	810,6	805,2	783,6	759,7	738	719,2
Luxembourg	62,2	67,6	68,7	70,3	72	72,9	71,4	72,8	77,1	75,8	77,2	78
Hungary	1855,1	1879,4	1905,6	1924,2	1945,5	1968,2	1988,2	1976,3	1952,2	1916,1	1873	1824,5
Malta	:	78,1	77,6	77,9	77,1	78,6	81,1	79,8	78,1	74,8	74	75
Netherlands	3136	3122,6	3171,1	3217,3	3208,1	3238,9	3264,1	3289,2	3317,5	3345,5	3379,7	3402,2
Austria	1426,1	1442,9	1458,8	1463,6	1422,1	1429	1452,4	1461,9	1470,8	1457,3	1467,8	1468,8
Poland	8866,8	9002,6	9073,8	9152,5	9153,1	9077,3	9004,3	8887,4	8663,4	8416,3	8168,4	8007,6
Portugal	2076,3	2019,5	2032,3	2002,4	1963,6	1961,5	1945,3	1913,1	1862,3	1881,1	2108,6	2161
Romania	4019,8	4006,4	3962,1	3954,2	3938,5	3914,7	3900,7	3847,4	3831	3839,4	3903,5	3879,2
Slovenia	385,5	391,5	389,4	403,3	407,1	407,7	411	409,5	403,1	394,8	387,9	381,2
Slovakia	1122,9	1119	1122,8	1114	1108,5	1104	1107,7	1101,3	1088,6	1079,4	1059,4	1034,6
Finland	1100,6	1125,5	1152,3	1171,7	1178,8	1192,5	1206,3	1239,9	1246,4	1251,3	1251,3	1236,7
Sweden	1961,9	2075	2089,5	2106,9	2114,8	2118,8	2122,5	2113,8	2096,1	2060,6	2022,8	2028,2
United Kingdom	13232	14835	14955	15038	16407	16043	16550	16714	12736	12607	12671	12780
Iceland	71,3	71,6	73,5	74,4	76,8	80	82	83	84,3	85	86,6	87,2
Liechtenstein	:	:	4,5	:	:	5,9	6,1	6	6,2	6,3	6,3	6,4
Norway	957,8	980,8	989,3	993,2	1005,2	1036,2	1052,4	1052	1068,1	1078,9	1077,5	1080,7
Switzerland	:	:	:	:	1294	1314,8	1330,2	1333,6	1340,4	1349,8	1355,1	1361,3
Montenegro	:	:	:	:	:	:	:	:	:	:	:	:
Croatia	:	:	:	:	:	725,2	730,1	735,9	732,6	728,1	722	709,7
Former Yugoslav Republic of Macedoni	378,8	383,4	385,6	386,6	384,9	381,2	376,8	374,4	366,3	368,5	385,1	377,8
Turkey	:	13571	13169	14893	15389	15565	16379	16021	16275	16687	16649	17471
United States	61816	62795	62323	63653	64440	65738	66075	66597	66793	67429	68041	68685
Japan	21368	20908	20583	20254	19956	19646	19435	19218	19095	18885	18658	18517

http://epp.eurostat.ec.europa.eu/tgm/download.do?tab=table&plugin=0&language=en&pcode=tps00051

Appendix: A6

Crossing boarders - Cooperation for a strong united Europe

A total number of 144 people answered the survey. Disparities may rise of people skipping some questions.

1. General Information

a) **AGE**

until 17	0	
18-20	0	0,00%
21-23	72	50,00%
24-26	55	38,00%
26 or older	17	12,00%

b) **SEX**

Male	53	36,00%
Female	91	64,00%

c) **COUNTRY**

Hungary	144	100,00%

d)

RESIDENCE	Total	Percent
Borsod-Abaúj-Zemplén	144	100,00%

e) **PROFESSION**

Student	127	88,00%
Employee	17	12,00%
Supervisor	0	0,00%

f) **BUDGET**

- 65.000 HUF	102	71,00%
65.000 HUF - 90.000 HUF	0	0,00%
90.000 HUF - 120.000 HUF	20	14,00%
120.000 HUF - 160.000 HUF	20	14,00%
160.000 HUF -	2	1,00%

g) **Do you have a part-time job? (Only if you are student)**

Yes	24	17,00%
No	120	83,00%

h) **How many hours do you work in your job? (Only if previous question was "Yes")**

- 5 hours/week	72	87,00%
5 hours - 10 hours/week	0	0,00%
10 hours - 15 hours/week	0	0,00%
15 hours - 20 hours/week	0	0,00%
20 hours/week -	10	13,00%

i) **What is your function in the company?**

Easy support work	6	25,00%
Advanced support work	6	25,00%
Leading role	0	0,00%
Other	12	50,00%

2. Education information

a) **Level of degree**

Highschool or comparable	24	17,00%
College or comparable	120	83,00%
Other	0	0,00%

b) **Which faculty are you signed in?**

Economy	46	36,00%
Law	46	36,00%
Mechanical Engineering	35	28,00%

c) **Year of graduation**

2010	42	33,00%
2011	42	33,00%
2012	42	33,00%
2013	0	0,00%

d) **Please select the skill matching for you in the following matrix.**

(1 = no knowledge; 2 = basic knowledge; 3 = intermediate; 4 = advanced; 5 = fluent)

	1	**2**	**3**	**4**	**5**
English	0	0	72	48	24
German	24	96	0	0	0
Hungarian	0	0	0	0	120
French	96	24	0	0	0
Italian	72	0	24	0	0
Spanish	96	0	0	0	0

e) **Did you visit a foreign country during your studies?**

Yes, I have. Only holiday.	48	33,00%
Yes, I have. I was studying abroad.	72	50,00%
No, I haven´t.	24	17,00%

f) **Are you planning to spend a semester abroad?**

Yes, I want.	72	50,00%
No, I don´t.	72	50,00%

g) **Do you intend to live abroad after graduation?**

Yes, I want to leave the country.	120	83,00%
Yes, but not permanently.	24	17,00%
No, I want to stay.	0	0,00%

h) **What kind of job are you looking for after graduation?**

Internship	48	33,00%
Operative or support staff	0	0,00%
Supervisor	24	17,00%
Manager	48	33,00%
Start own business	24	17,00%

3. **Education and Employment system**

a) **Do you think your university encourages and supports students to go abroad?**

(1 = does not apply; 2 = insufficient; 3 = sufficient; 4 = good; 5 = excellent)

	1	2	3	4	5
Information system about studying abroad	0	29	29	86	0
support in advance	0	0	58	86	0
support during the time abroad	0	0	58	86	0
support for the time after return	0	28	58	58	0

b) **Are you satisfied with the facilities and staff of your university**

(1 = does not apply; 2 = insufficient; 3 = sufficient; 4 = good; 5 = excellent)

	1	2	3	4	5
Knowledge and skill of teachers	0	0	29	58	29
Amount of provided equipment	0	0	115	29	0
Condition of rooms and equipment	0	0	120	0	24
Schedule of the classes	0	29	34	88	25
Standard of classes and exams	0	0	34	84	26
General support of the office	0	58	20	37	29
Offered courses	0	29	41	74	0
Access to service-points	29	0	88	27	0

c) **How much time do you spend researching for upcoming events in your field of study?**

- 2 hours/week	115	80,00%
3 - 5 hours/week	29	20,00%
6 - 8 hours/week	0	0,00%
8 hours /week -	0	0,00%

d) **Does your university help you to find a job after graduation?**

(1 = does not apply; 2 == insufficient; 3 = sufficient; 4 = good; 5 = excellent)

	1	2	3	4	5
Offering information days	0	0	86	30	28
Offering specific vacant jobs	30	28	48	38	0
Offering bill-board for information	0	51	93	0	0
Offering newsletter in any way	29	30	59	26	0

e) **What reasons are lead you to leave the country?**

(1 = does not apply; 2 = insufficient; 3 = sufficient; 4 = good; 5 = excellent)

	1	2	3	4	5
There is no future perspective here	31	0	37	0	45
I want a change in climate (quality of life)	0	0	41	13	44
New challenges/beginning	0	31	27	60	0
New environment/people	0	39	26	25	28
Higher salary for job, better social benefits	0	0	0	0	144

f) **What reasons could make you stay?**

(1 = does not apply; 2 = insufficient; 3 = sufficient; 4 = good; 5 = excellent)

	1	2	3	4	5
Improvement of job situation	0	36	72	0	36
Increasing the salary	0	36	0	88	20
Better social benefits	0	44	31	36	33
Improvement in working conditions	0	75	0	0	71
Political reasons	72	38	0	34	0